D1625557

ISBN 1-882022-17-3

Distributed by:
Small Press Distribution, 1814 San Pablo, Berkeley, CA 94702
Inland Book Company, 140 Commerce St., East Haven, CT 06512
The Segue Foundation, 303 Eighth St., New York, NY 10009

O Books
5729 Clover Drive
Oakland, CA 94618

Price: $10.50

The drawings on the cover are by Robert Grenier, traced for color separation by Leslie Scalapino.

SUBLIMINAL TIME

Milton Apache 97 / George Albon 65 / Laynie Browne 5
A.A. Hedge Coke 35 / Norma Cole 56 / Jerry Estrin 66 /
John D. Greb 72 / Robert Grenier 45 / Carla Harryman 83 /
Lyn Hejinian 83 / Susan Howe 32 / Lizbeth Keiley 12 /
Lori Lubeski 91 / Laura Moriarty 29 /
Eileen Myles 98 / Jena Osman 19 / Randall Potts 70 /
Aaron Shurin 15

O/4

O Books

Introduction: *SubliminalTime* , for Jerry Estrin, is a collection of writings by eighteen poets.

Laynie Browne's question "How is it that such thin lines can catch a voice" refers not to the speaking voice, or 'voice' in the conventional sense of 'finding one's voice'; rather, an interior articulation is 'in the middle of the writing', and so in a sense not in one: "To converge at a point in the matter which fills a body out of mind." One is a blindspot which begins at the mouth. As in Lori Lubeski's corpses aroused, intrepid, moving alone, *no* world is from a strong boyhood dream.

Browne's writing is also deliberately a blindspot which makes only a "relational proximity." The identity of one is highly vulnerable by being "inside of this picture" which is only in language. One isn't either the body or in one's mind: "The function of a knee; for wading into subliminal time." Lubeski's "The bloodhound eyes / inset a criminal mind forever the capillary": dream causes space for the mind criminal to be amused. It is the Persian Gulf, our country.

Jena Osman observes the text to create a level of it being dead, similar to Browne's "relational proximity," where the text is purely its own center of gravity: "This is from *my* memory...A pendulum is no longer itself. Once it has stilled, the clock ends and there is no relation between action and life."

Osman's making a relational proximity of a man severely beaten on camera and her memory. History is subliminal time which can only be apprehended in the writing, which is dead in the sense of giving up making connections, which negate its apprehension: apprehension is the event then.

Converging point (of the writing) is being inside of the man being beaten, which is entirely different from the conventional description of/as fiction. Writing as that convergence is a "letter that he cannot gesture." That letter that cannot be gestured is 'history' being in the 'present' as in Susan Howe's *MelvilleMarginalia*, Norma Cole's excerpt from *Rosetta*, and Laura Moriarty's 'novel' fictionalizing Queen Elizabeth and Mary in the age of exploration. Moriarty's 'novel' is a configuration of their thoughts/features 'as if' their minutia. History is meeting with fiction at the point of their construction (the writing).

The self-conscious viewing of 'history' as being a 'view' of it, double-edged, is evident in A.A. Hedge Coke's writing which is aware of ('the outside's' delineation of) Native American or Indian and it is being that; comparable to Robert Grenier's 'poems' drawn superimposed on each other so that their meaning and reading are the same in that imposition.

It can *only* be from being that, in that sense is 'history', as 'we're' opposed to analysis becomes the means of the superimposition.

Extensions sprout out of sources that are not their origins, occurring everywhere. Milton Apache's writing causes originless connections. It gets to where nature is being seen as originless: "night falls followed by day break." Aaron Shurin's "Human Immune" hallucinates nature. As if it were blind.

Similarly, Lizbeth Keiley's writing projects 'interiority' as convergence with one's surroundings, in a dual erasure/imposition of one: "My parents were illegitimate basset hounds." It is a form of hallucination, which is accurate. That era- sure 'culturally', which is everyone's, and as literally death of 'others' from AIDS is the act of realistic hallucination in Shurin's "Human Immune." Being in that space of 'everyone's' is akin to enmeshing of Robert Grenier's 'poem' "I am a beast/ my heart is beating," the two lines inextricably superimposed visually. Nature is a blindspot, and writing is.

In George Albon's "Cosmophagy," text is "a kind of pre-planned operative music,' a "parting intensity" so that (asking the question "what is history?") observation can "move the opposite way at an identical rate of speed". The sense of time in Jerry Estrin's "Brace", is akin to this pre-planned music as to Osman's dead text. In "Brace," Roger Maris's act (of the ball game) is stillness: "I am finished. I will be visible forever." History is where there is no relation of action to life, and therefore event is brought to both as if retrieved backwards where it's 'only' cognated: "Crowds intensely draw all stories to themselves."

Eileen Myles's "The Poet in the World" was delivered as part of a campaign speech in her candidacy for president of the United States in the recent election. Her childhood, her being gay here, the self-conscious relation to her dog as a delicate balancing that is 'one's' 'style,' the prefiguring of the deaths of others from AIDS which have already occurred around her, are the political representation alone; the voice (of the speech) is the image/'name' of herself, the existence of the 'life' of the 'poet'. She is her voice there as she runs for president, perishable. Randall Potts' writing makes objects become the spaces filling them, a double sight where images are absent: "Each body alone in the clearing pierced." Sight of events occurs before or after them, so one is in the middle of their occurring: "Trees in the foreground radiant / In reaching wind events bluish too slowly."

Lyn Hejinian and Carla Harryman's collaboration has a simultaneous "we" or "our" in picaresque erotica mirroring the 'novel,' the form of which is now dead. The dual convergence makes that form dead where they're playing afterward. Similarly, John D. Greb's text is "My own place a blur camera" in which he is to "expand the inhibition till it breaks." "Retreat is sublimation" in the sense of a convergence of the self with plotless excess: "Linear thought is incomprehensible that is why things are like this. This is why these words have thoughts that connect. Only because I say so. Is this my novel?"

Hejinian and Harryman's project, collaboration as such, makes fun of inhibition in not sticking to the 'subject.' There can't be a uniform subject created by dual memory. Grenier imposes images that are writing over each other ('poems') which are read as that imposition only, as if the intellect were feminine and it is in the (American) wilderness. Howe is making a history present time, in a sense out of no materials as a form of dual memory: "A polyglot anthology / out of no materials / is absolute derision". Norma Cole regards the letter, writing, (of the Rosetta) as singular, before us, our memory. John D. Greb's 'self' is the blur camera of a dual memory of erotic communications that cross poetry.

The focus of this anthology is to present the writings of a selection of younger poets, A. A. Hedge Coke, Laynie Browne, John D. Greb, Jena Osman, Milton Apache, George Albon, and Randall Potts, in juxtaposition to works by writers of 'older' generation, which suggests a 'relational proximity' in current writing.

4

Laynie Browne

Sending the Lake
Part One: Separate Present

Leave means what winters a gown, and what has grown between the restlessness of lakes.

An object brings a visit, or she arrived to purchase a daughter. Sun lilts through cloud-windows. Pavement moves faster under simple-blue. It wasn't a shoe but the passing hour, and the sound of mentioning, and the sound of nothing to say.

A sleep shafted in the sleeproom where below the brightness of white sheets a prism wept. Refractions wet themselves. Without the glow inside the center sent away.

§

How is it that such thin lines can catch a voice? If you move often enough to fill one page in any year, you are barely resting.

The function of a knee; for wading into subliminal time. An occupation as a trick in the flow of days.

§

A blindspot begins at the mouth and continues to speak through the afternoon. Her hat lay on top of a pile of books. To be inside of this picture discharged the temptation to ask. Someone else must provide the foresight of the witch, ushering change.

§

One mis-bleeding, still past numbness years, is not more than one drop away. In the center of the carried disturbance lies one broken vessel, magnified to overshadow the rest of everything.

§

Evenings barely begin to reach the level of relational proximity, meaning weekends are needed for evolution.

The dress transformed until remembering the need of not being seen.

To converge at a point is the matter which fills a body out of mind. Travelling to reach there is the destination of a rainbow; a lapse from the usual designs of our legs.

§

What it means to be heavier is not what is held inside but the extent to which the surroundings press down upon the virtual form.

Ways to describe a form do not include a mirror or a pond but the vision and the pond, or the eyes lied down in the lake.

§

Without realizing the occasion, there are those who would invent removable laws, anything to bother the sanctuary.

To live without a phone promises other voices, and far from neutral, penetrating the will to go back.

Less and less present calls to mind one and one more to make of the elevator shafts and designs.

Darkness reads the signs and postulations of a separate present. All a question which must be filtered through such a young digesting system. With star-luck it is possible to reverse.

§

What can be kept is the notion of the girl with the garden, the interior regions of which are yet unmapped, or the map changes each moment, curling and uncurling its proximate edges.

What transpires to form a wave could appear in sound and the weight of past thought. Or nothing changes in a sand maze. Reaching a turn, you turn.

Growing up unlike the park. Two different issues, the crowd, and the self, both running. Thickness can be calmed and lengthened, but where the light falls, falls.

§

There is a summer carried.

Shattering the structure, the tower, everyone somehow leaving no orchestra.

Sage, saying, sent, messages.

It is the shell which is unimportant, movable hands.

§

A forum is not a skull. Catwalks and a descending cage, or crowns, in her third voice. Which gender appropriates those. We understood this heard through the door.

Abruptness, cloth-light, frame, sill, arch, palace scathed internal measure. Please skirt. Corner hung crooked from past state. Saved-cared, saved-cards, carved-safe, can-latch, fingers hear Gustav Klimt, congeniality spell thin and less liven. Pronounce, promenade, lemonade, list.

§

Remember said pressure in the middle of the night, and pulled a towel around shoulders in the strange house sitting on the bathroom floor. Apology hears what apology said, strained with a match and shifting weight tested to a full size week. Smaller than hands taken in and held that way.

§

Under eyes specific nodding away doors and burns the allergy walk between rows after late binge and answers the following alone. A hinge spins. Alter sides beyond the tied up trees and past the balcony ledge, through the radio, in the phone, dark voices through the wires wish to mend a trying, while the temperature has settled on the fan, and the man is more than this crustacean in a fist, bothered by the hall and piles of words and each simulated violent dream, as the walls lean in and a family becomes an object or a maze, meaning the bed remains lying down. I don't question stance as more than a position which is physical or tired as opposed to beaten. What glares is the silence of the reach, or the multiple nature of possible cures, and hidden documentation internal and drifting to decipher a series of locks.

Four keys are needed to enter the apartment, on a ring, tangible. He offered his with the apology that there was no home to accompany them.

On this ground you are grown, and on other growth stitches continue. Your head is a heavy object, carry it away and tell what else it lies beneath, to say patterns will always emerge. Comfort is communicable as all other diseases. There is a place where we can sink deeper and sleep and exaggerate the season with our glowing. A splinter has no real access under the skin. Do not pull the blanket from around my body, I am in chrysalis state.

§

Part Two: Means To Send

Precious resistance finds velvet and all return in wave-suits.

Stillness prescribes fathoms, the small inner ear rooms vanish into banquets.

§

A button taped to a door. Two o'clock planning. Two o'clock repeated. Fire drill, protruding up the stairs. Small sounds smaller. Sense that hand moves to the neck, a glimpse.

§

The smell of the street when once walking seemed personally owned. Destinations drawn with personal eyes.

A walking sidewalk faces sky, drifts midline towards the center of the screen.

§

Last embarked upon a usual throat inhabitant. Somewhat ash slanting across morning the Monday diorama.

A place which is not hollow may be hollowing inhabitants. Hollow by virtue of substance, by memory of obstacle.

Simple lights in windows pose questions. Florescent pacing pulled back. Drawn out of beds as sacks of movable rice, scattered to various tasks.

§

Dandelion gloves. Teeth transfer cinema. Fire escape lip.

Strings held at distances which parts consider desire.

§

He had no skeleton, his only means of support a microphone, and leather twine around his neck, connected to some invisible line which gesticulates, despite the lack of breeze.

§

Recursive pendulum. Underbelly flushed. Walked slowly from shower to bed to avoid cold. Rushes become downpours pulled apart in one room. Consumed elsewhere, the blond floor.

§

That the appearance manager disliked the flesh woman yet was attributed to mechanisms. Attire allowed some structural element to threaten the empire.

An appropriate exterior suggested nothing was placed directly in her box.

§

Categorize fluff, crutch, resistance without water or appetite as a plausible cause with body bent.

The desire to wander not part of a structure.

§

The man-woman charm at work emulsifies conditions of doubt, interference, or what they are saying being closed doors. Sealed and believed to be unconscious. Disagreement in a series of clicks.

§

Renovation might deny the larger structure, where the sink is not attached to the wall.

A fabric of relations might deny the larger structure, the smaller case of the cell.

What motivates navigation as an unseen draft; mechanism of the mind, in the hands of the earth.

Part Three: The Lake

Bit by drop, obstacle by particle, carried between two palms, up onto the shore.

§

Twilight fix. Suspended underwater, with wings and ink. Imagery despite the time, conjured from disorder.

One moment past many sachet and rising wake to dig.

§

Given a division. Pavement spins. Talking in sleep as an outlet, unable to channel the flow.

§

Spell morning given one leaf beside the bed. Subliminal churning or obstacles placed at feet to be parasitic wash.

Stained pomegranate ceremony. Watery eyes, a context changes. A monthly blur. The proximate signs.

Misbringing of the past to selves or hearing a different part of the words each time.

Dialogue, leaves, parting; skylight equation language.

§

Evicted from trance, certainty hinges at the hip.

Cohabitation in fields became curves.

§

Sought a tired trimmed, weary wanders landing, even the eventual rested all touch to climb.

Encompassing, the body speaks perched dry, clear-wet.

Surfaces informed are permeable. The bottom contains chants hear from inside the head.

§

A purpose is not a torch or any intended lack, as if gladness had a discernable face.

Days rain from fingertips. Others cannot be called to question, as in flames from pavement.

§

Hollowed and played against the weather, followed by a haunt.

Out of sync. A breech. Promise borrowed, procured. Invoked, doubled back, realizing the present also claims a variable.

§

The studied past does not behave with anymore predictable orchestration. This is not clairvoyant, but somewhere said inside one voice.

§

Blue messages appear in bone while sleeping.

§

Seasons not wilted but clockwork. Once thought on a pin fell off a necklace of fake nails. Under skirts and swimming, a pressure museum. She does not believe in madly in.

§

Where water calls a question, ripeness warrants a watery lack of separation. So that creature-from-shell is not the same as being-from-shell, so that the shell's being must be counted along with any inhabitants in documenting sources.

Lizbeth Keiley

HER STRANGER IN EXILE

How she spent her mind in the hours of its most tentative decay and rapture was only part of some larger, more meager plan. *"I'd been floating all this time, behaving like a sponge, a fortress, a treasure, a wave, a seabird. a harpsichord. some musical siren speeding into the heat, only to find. only to learn, only to come to know...*

NO ONE BRIEFED HER ON THE INTRICATE
SURROUNDINGS OF HER OWN MIND.

*"How do I limit
the stems of each fever
eating the palm of my hands,
memorizing my fingers
like some past ghost*

*who slides on my body
during the night
slamming me into the bed
with his knees*

*and forcing me to forgive him
afterwards. To pretend
he's just my father
in the morning."*

The doctor: You must spend the next year decoding the neuro-bops in the bifubula of your proverbial baseline apparatus and spill all the beans into this metal canister on my desk.

ii.
Words began
for themselves
ashamed in light
to be erased in sudden inextricable
moments
slurring off in the nearby town
and laundry.
In a brown-waisted leather basket
she was believable.

*"There are sensual hoops
in my mind. I believe in dreams being fathered to Jesus.
I of a ten hemming and having a rip to say."*

She had undergone certain changes that would appear in her sleep at a time when she was blank enough to understand them. *"My parents were illegitimate basset hounds. AS DOGS they were crowded in their small apartment on 10th street. I wound their suffering in a spool of yellow crayon and mistletoe."*

iii.

HER voice is stirophone-lemon squeezed. I have managed to sex myself to a pole where frogs are watching Christ and how to wipe out Finland. When I arrive home I begin to notice the skin around her thumb falling off and then the crackling halt of tender balloons tasting their helium. Such untamed remembering should certainly be kept IN A GARDEN OUTSIDE OUR HOTEL.

The men came later when we were still children. I had already been at the beach for days while her body brought a plastic bag to put the worms in. They were talking about catching A LOT OF THEM TO USE FOR BAIT. We hardly had ourselves for sandwiches much less meat for them to squeeze an opening for the worms.

Unravelling their long thick bodies before us,

WE ARRIVED IN LAW SCHOOL where no one in particular was hiding. The library log of names seemed to attract her pseudonym of Bah-hah blacksnake, member of the Neutral-Coats-of-Autumn organization. I then had the body of a female warlock: foreshadowing legs in sanguine relation to a topheavy mountainfarm. I combed several lace pillows with a three-dimensional mirror, hence the notes she began were riddled with lexical happening and sunshine in the barn of my six-shooter.

iv.

Looking in the backseat she knew I was uncanny in retrospection. Turning my head I saw her as a child, little blonde curls on her head, smiling. NOT KNOWING ME I WAS A CHILD THEN yet myself. For all the odd eggs spinning in cars neglecting the obvious signs of

HIDING under the public carpets, bent trees and swollen apples are no mirage for the season to unpack its titillating music. From the porch on the second floor I watched from the sky.

She was still a young woman
dwelling on death. Father
spoke to her on the edge of the porch
where she flung herself
off like a monkey. Father
was shocked and landed in a nearby tree. But then

SUSPENDED IN THE TREE

she decided she should have a baby. The test-tube sat on the mantel spiralling in brown botanical seeds. There in the leftover moonbrains of iii-reputed construction, the egg grew by day and by night.

v.

The children were younger now and full of excitement. With an axe she cut my feet in half. Giving me half-feet. I had so many thieves listening to my problem, one after the other with the name WINTER that we took the train on the floating platform.

Crowds pushing and discussing the ramifications of "poor dating rituals" made me feel at home - but he was a student of mine and she was trying to win the local beauty contest.

Her hair was dirty.
She was menstruating.
It was all wrong.
She was even borrowing other women's
maxi pads.
Father would be there to watch
always so proud of her
something   she had always wanted
from clouds that tumble and shift at the town,
curling, downward, raised in detail.
She knew of the beach, bathing, sipping
the fine cool air of mist and sun secluded in the sand.
These were my debts, my tribute to an old and avid stench
waning in my dreams. She became
prisoner to the stranger who lay buried
in another strife.

vi.

It was all a shattering sequence of marveled eyes and tombs that breathe. Each flower habitually wore another tag by its bed for emergencies. *"You keep telling me cider is warm, that you love my food, that you wish you could fling yourself into the applesauce, but I tell you it's all papermache like topaz skinny dipping in the mud."*

The doctor:
Surely your father's death
 will widen your heart
on his eve of holy water
and piccalilli slumber.
The curtains are breathing,
the table is shimmering

and the air is filled with potpourri madness
 made majestic in sin.

Funny how she noticed herself in shade light but never in the beloved death of a
funnybone in shivers. The funeral as beautiful - she enjoyed the golf flowers and the
certainty of CHRISTMAS COMING TO MEET HER with a mule of forgiveness.

*"All I ever wanted and needed and dreamed of and heard about and considered and
reneged on and told and stold again and hung and killed and washed and fed my
hands to the parking meter and brought my soul to the dishwashing counter and
sank my teeth into the dynamite factory is behind me. I plunge into the atmosphe-
ric darkness and no one follows."*

Aaron Shurin

Human Immune

I lie in your arms. I kiss your mouth. Use your nails, creature. Our roles —the crown,
the infractions — inhabit this sanctified place to the point of fanaticism. I have to
get my hands on the world.

Dead from complicity in San Francisco discharged me, the harp of a person had an
arc. Then listen to inhale the contagion, where in the trap of your consciousness you
have to pull to get out. Himself alone and scared kill mercies. The body has powers
to paint yourself purple.

And shifting grasses, such erosion and mosses, nightjars lived on the droppings of
sunny days... in that country of circumstances and moods — shattering its bark and
throwing pieces of it around. Facing away from the entrance, with jerky movements
kicking the sands backwards. I saw the size of a hand, losing hold of it...

Birdmen, across the rising hills and bay, rolling naked one night stirred and rose to
the spell. He's out there, into the dead stumbling mind. I'll be accounting for no
memory, without so much as a template. His nostril is hissing; his tongue in spasms.
He has several parts on a breeze, an asylum this story surrounded. The face ripping
wide open has led a team of men in white gowns and slow rhythm.

And twinges we ourselves devise woundingly by miscalculation — delicious
conflagration winking — to become familiar and to pulverize them all. Curves
could hope to find in this world no more beautiful hair. *Hell is round.* I squirted
them with kisses. On his back at the edge of the couch to die of pleasure, kneeling
into your asshole to form around me. Comprise our friends the memory of the
moments they passed in that virtue. Their honor therein, helpless before desire...

Where are you now, the harder you pull to get out? Then is that person fixing little sandwiches and watching TV? The Bay was fucked — ornate theories —there's the photo of "husband", hippies, Pt. Reyes beach, leering face, pink light, someone else. A portion of scripture, undiagnosed. The placement of objects is a language theme, no longer private. A little old hairless man had swollen up. Pain is healing me into submission, he wrote in his journal the secret of the universe: *hell is round*. You flop and thrash in fact.

The homecoming was marked and mapped; they circled in ever widening loops. Processions migrating on blue nectar — stopping in the rising air over coastal waters. I waited I repeated I waited the test. The results were not fooled. I spent the summer as a natural landmark —the bearer of delicate organs — leaving the destiny dormant on dry days — moving my wooden ship to research, under spell of the spray. The sun was gigantic, slow, low-hanging. We had to acquire some knowledge in this year, food for a narrative. Summer is short. Inquiry raising our eyebrows was contagious. Moonlight on meat.

He knelt down next to me — fallen giant, empty stump. Feeling the blood pulling around my thighs, "I think it's screaming," I said. He stood barefoot, one warm leg, nest at the belt, pink wriggling sack, I wanted to run into the sun now, bristling muscular bulging animal sedated by his eyes. My body shook against him on a hot summer day, gushing to life, blood-filled, blood-dizzy. He rolled over onto his side, watching the men. A ruin. A patient. Overgrown so that the flat air had no answer. We floated in which the memory moving our bellies going dark have all taken flight — a cure may be possible — tell me what words mean — pleasure for a coffin: turn and enter your home.

The ghost which leads to burning incense on the altars of magical friends —these gods come upon gods which erects them — confections of the deific —showers down events, the smooth operations of insignificant romances to penetrate into their historian's hearts and foist upon the reader authenticity of the marvels... At last he dies, this exceptional man who loves them, phantom spawn, fraudulent cures, boundless poverty and the images of objects. Just a while ago I gave you attentions pure and simple. I take the oath worthy of your friendship exterminated in me. The lancing pain stuffing me with bucks and thwacks to distill soul's fuck: slip away, leave the rest to me, initiated into our mysteries....

With the Sixties the Seventies in Berkeley shot forward for replay to put the spaces where he wants —stars in the universe suggest metaphysical poets — lingered in remission studying the cosmic characteristics of T-cells. Triumphant skull in the grin of his malady, whacked as he was in a feedback loop. It's necessary to interpret men compared to sleepers in a private world. Two men pass through a forest which passed for the real world. From the cardiac ward through the underground corridor to encounter arrhythmia on the cathode screen. His head, his heart, a wave-form. And he spoke his monologue directed outward from the wisdom of a body: *hell is round*, the little clay pot locked up. The dream-time of heroes trying to throw-up names: California, Parsifal, Chuck...

Night fell and a moon showed up between peaks. We were given a welcome for centuries. Aroused by smell in their human behavior a growl in heat, with a mixture of affection and respect. A little whipping, a little touching it lightly. One sometimes hears the ice snap with a seam in the center; large numbers breeding in our district at those breathing holes. Members kill themselves, interested only in sugar. Suddenly the door was flung open, a youth tumbled in; the event we'd been preparing for changed our life entirely. To wake up to stop the alarm clock with one hand I lay on my right side facing my other — my Other Side — pressing the human places in a firm grip that woke us up in horizontal posture turned to face each other, covered with a thick blanket, the murmur of description, connected by an invisible rod as resistance fluttered back and forth.

The end of perspective, the proper shapes, blobs and pillars and singing minarets. You're a mess in the park. You're a willing dirty dog. With the sun disappearing a low fog tucked-up the air. I slept resting on the windowsill, stranger than birds. I used to be little but when we came back they were gone. Overnight to hear whatever was to be heard. With its overgrown boxed body jerking in perfect symmetry, this wizard — see what there is to see — bruised in deep breaths, and an archeologist invited down to watch. He'd like to go from the bay to the ancient golden hills into the earth unannounced and never saying where. It was like some mechanical body secretly unstrung leaving accretions of soft dirt and mud. He kissed his waiting hand with both hands. The warm competence of the finished parts as if such machines had meaning. Touching it, the thin shell, tucked-in facing the bay may lie quiet in the dusk.

A way is opened; my initiated companions go after. Each gave his confrere the pleasure of sensations, sprawled on the stone floor. Sucking a moment of suspense into calm to savor its entirety, the combination of prick and ass and mouth, an eternity in that delirium he'll lie in your arms. Common measure in homage to fitting company. We'll make a circle *(hell is round)*, I want that energy while speaking, place yourselves close by me, excessive behavior swell discourse in proportion, the carnal prosperity of an everyday affair. It ripens and is born, having provided circumstances. Made an incision running around the head, then removed the strip of skin. Your body, the altar, on the altar. Go consult the children of love. There are minds, my friends, certain spirits, having rid themselves of vibrations, having progressed from extravagance to the speeding star, plagued in whose name passion alone dared multiply. Come — this'll serve as a bed — fuck my ass into my mouth.

This is what the dream referred to as *hell is round*. When he got out of the hospital it had the effect of wiping out history. Right now, the city was in intensive care, locked-out behind him. In the small room huge eyes flaming. His fried mind projecting on each side a sword to conquer — through the sense organs through the rain through the ward through the trembled fields of flowers as if shape had no substance through the living information completing itself. The blood of communion turning is a strange sentence. It broke through and fired experience at his head. Penetrated man penetrated himself. He was dragged through his address book deconstructed as official documents —the only way open. A limbo in lymphoma contemplated itself: he lived it, he loved himself, would love that too. He saw it spread out among us, pulled from his body. He could hardly wait to abolish himself, freeing him to go commando saving people, glommed onto another pretext in grief and love through the magical powers that underlay all his saved-up strategy...

I have variations about what was there: fathers, sons, and grandsons. When the sky cleared the weather superimposed corrections, noticing and recording more details. Fly to an elevated lookout post. It's my intention to describe history at the place we left them. Populations of flesh caught in our net. Of their courtship, of their species: their back was connected to display-movements fading toward the warm neck, a pirouette. Small circles this ceremony for hours on end. About the organization of behavior: some of them visited me. Animal behavior in the summer of 1956, or '76 — embarrassing luxury — while we were floating on the shore or in the sea or under veils in quiet corners as the haze hanging behind us... Feverish outburst played havoc with their exact pose while sitting indoors, digging out of the morning for tests, returned positive results on the same day; distance... I've made a number of flights already — round flat discs —homing. Then my legs stopped moving altogether. Under the full microscope ferocity with nerve endings waiting I hovered, motionless, maneuvered into position.

I will see him standing, pounded, irresistible. In the dunes of my thick woolen sweater, dropped off along the western edge, panting through the indistinct sand, puncturing the middle of the farthest horizon, arms raised. Through the muscles of aching arms and legs opening on my back to the sea, wrapped in tangled sunlight staring beyond him. What I didn't think or say fill my mouth, the terrible mysteries of sleep and navigation. We're best friends ever since ever. I noticed you in class — my full attention — if given the opportunity stammering to encompass love stanzas. Have you smiled? — choreography! Are you wrapped around my waist? — cosmic winds. San Francisco the beauty can take a picture — the air around him. I lay there on the floor, dug into the trenches, throwing down his trousers, the root of bones and mud and blood. I suppose he once lived here, curled into the tails of my nightshirt. He walked past me in his undershorts, an organism. We are the owner of sight and speech. In the gray light west of the Great Highway: not even me. We sat in silence, a blanket covering his lap. If you flew by you'd see these impostors, vapors of tenderness. It could never be contained.

Jena Osman

I. "Dead Text"

Once again, the starting point is Kleist as he tries himself to determine the starting point called grace. As it is found to be lost, as it once was held and discarded, the starting point. Can I hold you says the man. Are you able, once lost, to be found, to be held. The man takes you into his arms like a heart burning out of the body, out of the heart runs gravity. As it was found, then lost, where now might it be found? This is the question as posed and answered by Kleist: the center of gravity, the pole of the heart is to be found surrounded by dead text — "pure pendulums."

The sphere of a pendulum is limited to the utter purity of its scope. This is from *my* memory. A movement that continues, only in that once it has ceased, it is no longer itself (to be found in his arms). A pendulum is no longer itself. Once it has stilled, the clock ends and there is no relation between action and life. Thus, the dead text begins in the realm of the man with no consciousness who has something in his arms. This is the part that steps out from the outside.

The partner turns the man a falterer. Constantly losing his body as in Beckett, and addition indicates the opposite of grace.

"To fill a Gap+

+Plug a Sepulchre" [Dickinson]

Letters in the printed word are the man with "the stump." The pure pendulum of the arm is denied and the center of gravity changes irrevocably. Letters in print lack physical gesture, the arms enfolding. And then what do we produce? What is the nature of the gesture that we might endow? How do we construct the whole that will allow for the dead text, the weight and swing of it?

If your arm cannot attain that center of empty moves, you can attach a weight to a string which is in turn attached to your arm. The weight will solder the air and you can then say to the man, this weight is in fact my arm. If you do not do this you might falter.

Don't allow him the memory of completion. The lost limb must be on its own so that when he holds you in his arms he realizes your impossibility. And after, he is found on the front line, only to be lost in the letter that he cannot gesture.

Producing the arm that isn't there is creating the gesture that doesn't move (and in turn cannot produce?). As soon as the pendulum moves the moment is connected to another. Detachment (disconnectedness)—the picture—allows the man to see what's in his arms. The man is severely beaten on camera. Slow motion turns the act into moments, each swing has the possibility for justification for it is tied to the motivation of the last. He sees it is no coincidence that "scales of justice" are also based in a system of weights: however the centers are endowed (the half of the arm that is sense but not seen), placed artificially, a gap stopped with other: consciousness.

19

II. Theft Text [Defoe]

I stood in the pillory three times. Endowed with tools and materials from the wrecked ship. Indifferent city. Live on takings. To people a world. A real, physical world. I was diverted, I was instructed. My original. Original rogue fell a-crying. "I was a dirty glass-bottle-house boy." The dogs lick fingers. Nobody gets anything. Thou art a horrid doll, a kidnapped child. Now fill in the blanks and come to be hanged. Fires above, money in hand. The light is what lets you seem to live. Dexterous friends to lay there so still. What kind of trade has no interest in higher things? I was carried directly into the city and sold in a market of letters. Far from the world, my original. And never for a moment did they think but what are pockets for? To keep the bread from the dog. Vexatious ship, it was a heap of emp- brickbats. I knew not what I did, I know not what I do, in the hollow of a tree, in an ty pillory. Horrid doll (boy), a hat was a coach with six horses, now watch your steps. Around and over them, I jumped toward him and he fell. This was the grasp these people had of me. They are books and the boy is a pretty boy; a letter (what lets it seem to live).

III. Conscious Text

As the man was beaten on film, his center of gravity was lost and found in the mouths of the police. It is in that that the city loses its indifference. If the film is slowed to a pace of open interpretation, anything can be accounted for: the man was dangerous as Hercules. When a picture of fire is slowed down, stilled, disconnected, the man is dangerous. This is the paradox of detachment: in order to see, an image must be alienated from its usual context. When an image is alienated from its usual context, we know not what we see. The fire becomes beautiful in its photograph. The man is beaten and seen as fitting into some order. He has become dead in his attempts to stand, incapable of affectation. The mouths of the police claim the man was subject to affectation. According to Kleist the moment when all have attained the perfect grace of the dead text, the un-self-consciousness of the puppet, is the end of the world. He does not account for a time where a man is forced to be dead text and the others remain not so. He does not imagine a time where grace is the stance of the beaten. The relation between action and life depends on this.

Upbringing

"use the topography as the underlying skeleton on which to lay other things."

The skeleton of a building is accustomed to being a house
whether accustomed or usual
never leaning
like a leaf holding up a child
also able to float:
this is the puzzle of a man of low birth
and thus assassinated in a pail of water
where his body now rises to the surface

to count the rooms of the house
I will need some sort of calculator or weather vane—
this glass transom for instance
was convenient in the campaign
and a light not associated with societal bloom.
Sequester if you must, but understand the consequence:
neither life nor a more protected life will lead you
to that other life
if so, the body indicates
only as tea leaves once the water has been drained
the parts manufactured away from the site

I like when it becomes this color she said while looking out looking out at the air
which was yellow due to a storm let us blush home count it up. However I feel as if I
feel as if. Now the buildings are out of site, beneath the yellow and a ghost as if I
feel. Terrible terrible I said in response but unlike myself too this air not moving
enough inward and outward her breathing sequestered in a perception from the
window of her home. I like it when I can breathe she says in doing so but kept alone
in a tower in constant fear of isolation so as to populate to populate the room the
rooms with others one of which am I.

holding better branches out in the fist
an apparatus, a doll
held down into one world
recedes the flesh not far enough
from a desire
so the tubes of commutation
fill with iron, girders
the modern steel
which allows us to place the self
to one side of the self

mirrors arrange in a silver tray
dedication, a lair lamp
adore, *dream*
the brutal part of the feign
the sin error I am for
surly under the cadence
below but so north
vacant hour the edge of a core
approach through the alley
push the floor
maybe ruins of a counter hour
a few days there came and forgot

How necessary it must be, she said, to tip the scale in on its own neck and let only so much water find its way out into a part, a quality. I support the arid matter, she said, that only beats itself rag, churns out rough face or body got all the oil drop of a flame chart liquescent marry. How necessary it must be to adapt the scale, she said I'm my own neck I meet a drop of water near my way out of it my way of curing simple rages and cuts a trial rig to take you away from ceremony or inconsequence to reason the pair away from each parapet.

pastor pasture metal hand
see hear marvel
in accordance with a space closed in

the rain was mounted on levers held in coils on an old engine
action was slow
it first was revolved around a carousel holding letters
and played like a piano
the wind was employed in blowing the tickets
the letters were mounted on tickets
held by a man in charge of alignment
he was the heart of the machine
and believed in glass to enclose the inner working
and to render him "noiseless"
rain in the boots
hands thrown up in disgust the action
was slow they all could see it
his fingers hesitating on the coils

With the feet she said, with the feet leaving each one then done behind, the steps step, shipped behind the body. Next to nothing. The extended edges of the wheel, well, spokes, thirst. So much depends on a correspondence with the outer she said world. A dance step makes the flowers tremble. The voice is a system of deposits. She said. She said she said. Identify clamberers. They are fractured beyond an arbor, far from bone. And now here.

There never are more
than circles drawn
that quieter fit a calm turn
around never my ever wrist
a lunar disk
a gone replication of pursual
definite, not as a four-way mirror
wandering through and under gravity
a biological sphere connected to a radius
portrayed by a particular motion

tines

as
fingers
in the play that exhibits them
as articles up for auction
or are they simply bones
a small set of vertebrae around my wrist
caught up in representing something finer
shinier

Industry of Balloons

aeronauts one o'clock surgeon stop do start at the interior a point
                              the liver the lifeboat transatlantic
emplacement cutting from a height
                              the skin thicker, lighter, steam
whose ratio I couldn't know, a dream
                              vision imparts 64 overlapping gunfire
frames and shots, early steam on the ground
                              the enemy of balloonists: science
oxides, a landing in a tree, fights
                              the eye to turn blue then white
then not to see the entire area but cut
                              into numerous lights thrown
onto general incisions the wind makes you bleed
                              stop barrels sulfur washed and dried
interior domestic flight never built
                              a spare anatomy for advertisement
slim bridge of your feeling well denied
                               instrument inflated for crucial reports
in the upper left above the army
                              to carry apparatus my assistant my wires
I took another observation stop another look
                              there goes the last of it. envy
see what I cannot see none were shot down
                              of drummers for tall drums
more frivolous exhibits of the moon plants spectra
                              the palm is the polestar then
two images of the doublestar confuse my enumerations
                              because it looked as though we were banded
on the stairway up to the lens
                              but it was chemicals and a fine pencil
and an application of an image twice over stop
                              do stop and take a look: barrels drums
an empty star the eye is in
                              blue then white now black again
it was a revolution in light shot down

                    as oxygen combines with iron
and plays a loud band hydrogen bubbles through
                    in the shack on the ground see it
down badly broken the machine the operation
                    spins it over in the sand men to fly
fires to propel the air and sweep us up
                    some kind of race over the city, lighter
discarding to be lighter I throw my shirt over the side
                    the medicines the sandbags and drums
of sulfur but hide my ticket, know to do that
                    or else to cast out the center of my hand
the fair began by starting the engine
                    the hand made in France arrived safely
and the people stepped inside of it
                    psalm-singing purse-snatching
hand held nostalgia for days of family business
                     medicines remedies
caused a riot in the upper decks sandbags weapons
                    famine burglary shots these people
seem so small almost unreal when in fact
                    could it be the hand too large
and those markings giant stitches. shots
                    like we've rarely heard award
ether drift a mile downstream swimmer is incorrect
                    what does fill the spaces in between
practically zero when it is quiet
                    and unlike myself or rather too much
wireless thought flies in the face of cross river
                    down river take the drifting home
witness the world of change
                    sits still ballast brought
as a small brick falls from the roof
                    makes you think of the key
necessary to open the fence that lets you on the dock
                    knocks on a few doors the wind
lifts you up and diverts the brick
                    so that the planks can hold two men
lead directly to the doors and then he walks
                    further into it the solid part
that I don't see even though I try
                    energy unable to be transformed
heat death the fence is opened and I walk in
                    every note he took every formula
was everlasting, exalted as close as could be
                    the paper took shape a turbine wheel
so that the dock was more important

                        and the parties went quite late the water
and mirrors were to catch the guests
                        before the dive a mile off from the solid
always pushing it away we find
                        cuts the skin they forgot to cushion
the sharp ends that lift you up
                        before the dive I don't even try to see
the ether throughout an entire life
                        small difference between paths
the ballast we brought refused now always
                        in the pockets or heavens
were flooded out while looking for
                        a cheap illuminant scratch the face
a return to darkness household lighting
                        how might we light the face
with a proper price. coal distilled medicine
                        and the nose disappears with a blanket
soaking up the liquid I slip back behind you
                        not what I expected to see oil
that spoils the brine the town is now a wall of derricks
                        and that is what I see inside the mouth
that has dipped a small blanket in a pool of mud
                        its features disproportionate however equal
to the eagerness of the town

Odradek

Accurate spinnings and a body offshooting, making good on the turn, brake, commute, be there up on one wheel. This is accurate because we can see it. Then again, no.

As with a kit he is put together, a mass of loose ends. A dose of persuasion and fury allows the charge to act as speed, and thus, disappearing. Be forever in his presence and you, too, might build a bridge.

But there are no banks to either side.

At certain point, you, too, may be recognized for what you once were. Then again, no. He lives in a finely painted house in which a yard grows and where a dance goes on. Light on the feet, over the wheel, up the road.

The speeches lapse the eye behind into a previously hidden corner or closet. That's how we see. And through this cloudy glass we can make out his mechanics. They reach to resound and yet pull back *before* sound.

25

Gloucester sees—"I know thee well enough"—but first an evidence in a flash of light. What he once was is outside like a frightened bolt. He reaches in to greet it, casts it deep into a pocket, whirs to the other side. To continue with speed and to act as lineage. This is how he sees.

Lepsy

for David Lang

> *"...we live in a zone midway between
> things and ourselves, externally to things,
> externally also to ourselves."* Henri Bergson

on defects that laughter corrects

> You will rise ever over coal holder
> withdrawn with just a lever
> ...
> and now his eyes have wider grown
> so that the gears are never stopped
> the remainder of him following fast
> and alike to the road I followed him on

Once speech was considered a lapse of attention, and the lapse was considered amusing, in the speeches, once attended by the spectators that forget themselves.
§
as the street lamp (with pockets) runs through the cold
you barter
the way you
grew up
on irregular money

The comic effect is immobile; a glance errs in that it hits a rock and drowns. The speech was in fact a play attended by the spectators, provided with unsociable dreams. It was soon shot down by the man walking toward the banana peel.

across a coral floor, then crossed the palatial lawn
as like to follow
a human pattern where nothing
new is born
absolute stars that were a space between two roads
lapse, and he,
barely in sight with sounds,
into the grass I followed
§
Life forgets itself and turns rigid as an image; a natural rigidity in things as seen by the public, the audience of comic effects.

26

preparedness:
for example
ready-made operations
inverting the idea of good meant to be

we send a stick
through and on its course
a flexible vice
perhaps fathoms itself
a breach of propriety
composed of steps, rails
spartan arcs:

an industrial center, a phrase
inhabited by a river
attached to the parts that subside

sharp twist release
then watches itself
from one side spin

§
A pool stick can transform a person into a thing, a clacking jack-in-the-box, sur-
prising others at the corners, yourself from one side spins. The letter aims, strikes.
Don't sit down - you might spring back up like a clacking jack. Your clothes might
free themselves of their intended impressions.

trade self for character
uniform from any direction -
the bottom of the sea? - yes
all that sells, swims,
whisks a mouth up for air
(surveillance) - so that you are different (damage) whatever the cost

and the eyes grew out of *us*, "the man walking"

fifteen objects (effects) collide, disappear
necessitate a turn against the bank
furrowed color - wheels flat on their
sides, so in looking back

we fail their restoration
ourselves welded to the impassivity
of pictures

the inanimate no longer moves
beyond itself

into beauty filched
the character - first - once (a pleasure)
>>>>water floods the banks
>>>>in a confusion of tactile delight
>>>>and now the gears are never quite
>>>>the remainder of its following flight

>>>>>>>>collision, a carom,
>>>>>>>>does pitch both of us forward
>>>>>>>>although we fall in separate zones
>>>>>>>>into which we have run

§
There is a solution to the inattentive
dust. *This* constructs a relation to
said residue which continues to build and
is still, as such, labelled (for what it is).
Also an activity - some kind of search,
furtive and perhaps illegal in that
the object to be secured cannot be found,
much less named. Delight (the comic) is a means
by which society gives itself the once over.
A moral sound check. These givens set the
familiar poles. And now for a turn into
an untrackable direction or dimension.
Where the character is no longer marked
by habits...

§
he appears cylindrical

>>>>>>>>the character (the sailor) is a banker
>>>>>>>>of cue sticks and shells,
>>>>>>>>"a winner" although—

>>>>>>>>—hardly exhibiting life;
>>>>>>>>more a line drawn,
>>>>>>>>a connective, the web beneath
>>>>>>>>and above the table
>>>>>>>>that we seize before we move

Laura Moriarty

From: *Cunning*: Ned Bright

Lola went off with him, dignity intact. They had travelled across the Great Basin. It was the inland route. the overland trial.

"This sea," she thought, "is finite, except when compared to oneself. Then it is endless enough."

"'like gentle ridges of flesh proceeding down a belly not entirely taught tossing with breath so that I took her waist in both hands..."

She twisted away.

"The twelfth of August at six of the clock in the morning at last approaching the shore, I "Left the *Mermaid* at an anchor..."

He later became a locksmith and would have her join him there. but it was too late.

"And yet in some places else, I do otherwise shadow her."

The empty shells in ridges on the shore could be scooped up in handfuls. "and the frame of the bed was high all around. She broke through the plane of it with her movements as if to get over. I wasn't fooled, but worked against her will, as she would have me."

Saying finally, "You have left me nowhere else to go. The sense of inwardness overcomes me. I am defenseless. You are the same."

She came back.

In the woodcut the mermaid raises her hands in either a welcoming or dismissive gesture. The sailor floats or flies or falls among the repeated lines which represent water. The circles are waves.

It was her intention to break through the frame, the metallic skin she was imagined to be in. Elizabeth, the sharp knife. The law and The Tower were intimations then. There was every kind of Mary in those old stories. All of them secretly faithful.

Chrysopylae

It was called *Chrysopylae* (golden gate) on the map by the same principle that the harbor of Byzantium later Constantinople and finally Istanbul, was called *Chrysoceras* (golden horn).

I was emersed in the charts for awhile of that time and found some relief from my own.

Geographical Memoir

"My love, this book of letters has convinced me never to write another one. Realizing what was done. It was I that was done. I am firm about this. 'Hard.' as I saw written on the street, knowing it had nothing to do with us."

The inexorable progress of Mary's trial. The history of sisters. The court. The courtesans artificially called Lucretia. Each one a beauty. A blond melting in your arms. The honeyed one. Your head is groggy from long imprisonment there, The cold air filters in without impediment. The banishment. The flight from Egypt in what will become Nevada. The retelling.

And the trail. Sarah Winnemucca towers over it. The geometry Cheops transformed by the waterless mind of the explorer into a false name. They stood for something then. Belief. Betrayal. She and her sister married. They were of the Paiute tribe. They wore the fashionable clothes of their time. She addressed presidents and kings. Her speaking was robust. You can imagine the use of it.

The flight is depicted in a contemporary holy card. The card keeps your place in the sacrifice. It means getting ready to die, but not quietly.

The invisible storms in the lake took drunken sailors by the throat getting rid of them. Their terrible noise disturbed the blank.

The walls go yellow at dusk. Here it is autumn. One is deceived by the continued hotness of night and then breathless cold. It comes on suddenly.

In the morning are other walls of heat. Ouinn explained the gaps in her recorded speech any way he could. He wrote out his love. He fell in love with himself again in words. He kept it from her in case she would stop him. She would not have. Jealousy, even of words, was foreign to her. But she terrified him. He thought her too freely given. He found her silent as the waves of the local ocean. It was easy to be brushed by them. But this was not the past or the future. He was too familiar with her passion to allow it access to him now, even for a moment.

El Nino was said to be returning. The devine child of tropical rain had once lodged himself over the city like an angel nailed to a stable. In the time between the two droughts, the streets had run with him. Insignificant streams were swollen beyond recognition. He would never come again. Or he was a bright child on his willful way back to us.

The Circumnavigation coincided with Elizabeth's middle years. She was given to energetic uses of men and horses. The Oueen preserved her pallor with a mask. She powdered and covered herself with a glaze of egg-white. She mixed her own paint. She smelled of marjoram.

Ouinn existed in this context. He read and returned. He was read. Each time there was less of him.

He danced well if roughly. His handling left her breathless. Or it was the memory that left her. The country was named and abandoned. He imagined it was like home. Califa. Califia. She was an island of women long ago described and claimed. "They lived," he said, "with animals." "They slept," he wrote, "with gold."

"Sharp mountain ranges and naked plains cover the place. We will surely come to other collections of water, not yet known."

High and Dry

"I write under your threat."

"If I could do anything to stop it, I would do that thing. Or perhaps the desire itself, the pain of it, has a value, is an emblem."

"My life on the ship continues," she wrote, "though we have long ago arrived."

"There is no question of it. There is no going there, no there to go to. As much as it seemed to exist in the past. it did not. There is no substance to it in the present. No steady horizon. But it was the overcoming of mere fact that was always at the heart of us. This being false to oneself or true. It is impossible to tell, to resolve, or to forget."

The landscape looked both naked and hidden. She could see it rise up over her and reveal itself and yet had no idea what the mountains were called, what had caused this great incursion of water, or how far it went. It might go very far.

Mary continued to fight a war that had been lost. She trusted the wrong men. She allowed her view of the world to be skewed by them.

Elizabeth wrote letters. She wrote laws. She wrote on her clothes, on the walls. She argued in Latin. She danced in Italian. She vanquished the Spanish, massacred the Irish. She prospered and expanded, but, in body, shrank eating small irregular portions while her courtiers consumed the world.

We talked about elements, the elements of the situation, the story, the material. Mary would describe the world and I would redescribe it. She would agree silently, only to add a word which changed everything.

Mary was direct. Her directness was compromised by her need to hide her motives. She never admitted her part in the betrayal even to herself. "She has used me ill,' she was able to say at the end.

And so I continued to languish there, land in sight, but not on land. Writing and reading my book. It was about the past and yet also seemed to be producing the state that I was in, insofar as I was anywhere.

Susan Howe

Extracts from *Melville's Marginalia*

I like to be stationary. --Bartleby

Roosting on a ladder
for several months
even several years
the librarian Mangan
roved through languages
an unearthly figure
in a brown garment
The same garment
to all appearances
which lasted until
the day of his death
The blanched hair
was totally unkempt
The corpse-like features
as still as marble

§

Instead of classifying
he browsed and dreamed
he didn't even browse
regularly

§

He was not the polyglot
he pretended to be
Translations were the rage
of the moment
and he turned them out
as regularly and as competently
as he had turned out
acrostics some years before
From 1837 onwards
Mangan deluged
the Dublin University Magazine
with "translations"
from the Turkish Arabic Persian
Welsh Coptic Danish French German
Russian Spanish Swedish Frisian
Bohemian

§

Ask not nor task not
A polyglot anthology
out of no materials
is absolute derision
What nondescript yell
in reasonable Bohemian
and if the Modeem of
Alystan be kith or
kin of mine let dust
derange so ever darker
the glory of my hair
Simile is always poetry

§

I hate scenery and sun
half-whimsically if be
If I be clear what is Moore
derision half-seriously
House if the reader please
hovel to his originals'
What is a parenthesis.
Long passage on fallacy
hypochondriasis despair
the "Sarasenic world" &
Ind & other Ottoman airs
On the field at Mallach-brack
my shibboleth is refrain
Put my black wig back on

§

Sect him I cannot
to go skin deep two
in his triune cloak
for selfsame Selber
a German derivative
the poet-Cain's crime
Dash to the right Kathaleen
Ny —is the feminine
Mr. Editor you took
the part where four
roads meet Scattery
Drumcliffe Ratoo —My
grief to you Kilroy
Penny submission Aladdin

§

He rode his hobby a
round Fagel Library
unallied unhousel'd
under the Poor Law
My mind has no home
the dead face orient
I will "do" the song
out of the Jacobite
Counterfeit when you
look artist of Sais
My mind is its Cain
a semiocomic Paradox
Pun someone someone
Cimmerian garden Aladdin

§

"A sea of argument stretches out
before us
and the waves thereof curl
about our feet
But we forbear to plunge in
Reflection recurs
and we receive a *check*
on the *bank* "

Typological disdain of human applause
is the only great thing
about him

34

except his cloak
he said of his home-made poet
'Selber'

§

The longevity of the Irish
how Saints Mochta Ciaran
Brendan in a time of fast
reply a little bit of meat
Shrine doorway tower ruin
Drudge dole pauper famine
I too have been a dreamer
and am seeking a spiritual
leader on the ground and in
air out in perpetual weather
Regions of Araby the blest
royal descent for all of us

A. A. Hedge Coke

Pine Ridger with a Lambourghini Dream
for cante skuya mi

Ricochet you Pine Ridger with a lambourghini dream
share with me this insight   this exquisite   invisible rainbow
stretched before this South Dakota truck across postcarded southwest
where I develop affection for curvaceous narrow road
almost abandoned to romance by   haunting recollective psychotic alcoholic
          episode
they moved the mare that captured me between those highway maps'
          insignificant color lines
she's gone but somehow you and me get *somehow*   we linger on   together
capturing innermost desirous feelings
fleeting   always   fleeting *in a special kind of way*   they endure
look the single star to the southwest lighting the night sky
over the fiery sundown horizon cedar and juniper blackened by loss of reflection
drop night shade to dark cobalt to midnight blue unaffected by
emerald go lights   or caution amber hills darker without tungsten
outshining stars against the pitch of sky   spaced   matched equally
black black light   blacklight   bugcatching device
black to conceal to reveal you shimmering black sea   pin-pricked holes spark
          shimmer
cottonwood creating lace patterning webbing alcoves space in between more
          branched lace

35

across yellow orange moon   ridge across this path pathways to parts of me
I honestly forgot existed   the most secluded and denied essential components depth
        me
willingly drawn   shades open   by chord   your mood evokes
to dwindle only you   I spin the hydraulic tool   the jack you drug   out   changing
        blown out Firestone
alongside woven wood   branches   wire warp pueblo fencing   we swerved toward
while my pen covered contemplation   one boy's braid flowing past his narrow hips
kicking gravel   the other attempting performance macho   masquerading
        mechanical knowledge
both cold, tired   jet black   surrounding over, above, and across   sparkle and
        surrender lighting
automotive lamps passing   offering solution to dilemma   somewhere near Cundiyo
        and so on
the nearly 4'4" mechanic younger boy   who originated the Lambourghini dream
        stooping low
beside you "Watch the traffic" I beg and return to pen   on the blue seat of the
        white and black truck
much better than the older Datsun with formica and plywood floorboards that
        flooded out over rain filled potholes
currently without the familiar fear of frostbite in the colder months approaching
        fast
already the brilliant casts of snow dusted lower slopes remind us   mountains
        without fear   further without the
fear of exposure caused alcoholic frozen death grips   unless, of course, we
        surrender to fixate certain   relapse
tendencies attributed to lifestyle atrocities   freely now made into a give-away
        we no longer hold dear
 nor cling to   shimmer slow into   this night falling   into this clearing cross-section
        in our individual paths
in night without fear   without solitude   yet comfortable   belonging   glimmering
        sparkle shining by   breathe

Sidelays Gwance

Noose slips
swings loosely
preceding
White Man's lodge
Again the
megalamania
mediacentric
flash   snap and tape
documenting
documented peoples

those peoples registered
to the Department of Interior
along side
wild life,   wild-er-ness
those wild   people
refusing to remain
under pacification
undermining dominant
society's dogma
mining,   always mining,
Again reversing   throw
bark to blade
relocating,   reallocating lives
attempting snare
spirituality snare
their game denied
she dangles by
jawline   strangle vine
accepting new road death
rather than selling
ghosts to hosts
claiming new age obligations

Pasturing

Extensive wrapping
tables, falls, boughs,
shoulder joints and precipice.
Itching cloud and plummeting
far underneath the realm
of stimuli perception.
Unattainable measure on
shoe with rope probability.
Home accommodating that
snow which has desire
to linger further expectation.
A soaring universe dedicated
to wing flattened and spread
caressing breath along flight.

State of Invisability

yellow leaping arrows
expanses
ribs brushing space
emptiness
the vast void
filling draped skeletal
fashion
herein, the quickened
body sheltering
pezsnija sparks
wokalyapi hour
closer to rise
morning star reach
rattling on deep in
to the night
awaiting dawn
that break of day
forming a line,
blue-white light
on the very border
horizon   to the sun
to the east
to the world
we occur in
and I disappear
forever into crowds
by turning
intentionally to
remain anonymous
save splash
colors and
inked pages   torn
to   spread like a fan
to all directions
rippling back the stream
restlessness
meandering minds
holding   then tossing
candle light   back to
kerosene glass   with
wicks left while
surfacing lonesomeness

Legacy

(A performance piece) for Chris
Apache, Chris, Mike, & Lisa
Brooks, Art Harvey & James
Luna in 1992

Surviving in the post
traumatic era in
the dark ages following
the systematic genocidal
encroachment of the
displaced invaders,
intruders, currently occupying
and implementing martial law
throughout the western hemisphere

RLH
All you eastern hemisphere
people   are   just alike

They expect us   to believe
Europe and Asia are   NO ADC
separate continents
and that we walked across   NO BIA
from over there
or   that   space   NO CIB
invaders built our
pyramids and
medicine wheels   NO SERVICE
for us

RLH
Good thing we had
fish on hand
you might have
starved

So, your ancestors
were fresh off the
boat, huhn, the
Mayflower, huhn,
mine were here to meet them

Dehl Berti
Smallpox, measles, typhoid,
T.B., syphillis — all of

these   we acquired
in exchange for
a pair of glasses

Hudson Bay Blankets
            &
Hudson Bay Rum

Booze, alcohol the
slow smallpox blanket
we are still trying
to uncover its
disastrous effects

Ban the Booze in
Indian Country
Abolish the slow trade
blanket

That old man you called a drunk,
            dirty, Indian
is my father.   He never did take
the drink you poured down my
throat.   Your manager said he
could get these boxes in the
alley   to pack some   thing in
            h a t
we are moving. That man has a
            college education. He
grew up in a dug out,   in the
            1920's.
He fought with honors in your
            World War II.
He went to medical school riding
fence to pay   in Grand Forks
            before there was an InMED.
            He
worked for your Agriculture
            Department, for your
Helium Research, for your NASA,
            for the
E.P.A.   until you gave him
bronze medals and claimed we
no longer needed environmental
protection.   That man knows
our old ways and your new ways
            that you   yourself
are too slow and stupid to
grasp. You'd better watch who
you call dirty and drunk that's
my father.   He bathed in rivers

                                                      while
                                      you powdered yourself to hide your
                                                      smell.

It's a computer pow wow
Japanese Apple MacIntosh
Hey, What's that?
Hey, come check this out.
What is that?
Hey, this pow wow's
points are added up
on a lap top computer.
Looks like a toy.
Hey, get over here.
Dancers be on the floor
at 1:30 MacIntosh
Time. No, not Indian Time.
Japanese computer time.
Grand Entry at 1:30
MacIntosh Pow Wow Time.
Institute for American Indian Arts
Thirtieth Anniversary   1962 - 1992
Spring Celebration Pow Wow
I hear that the Writing Majors
protested for these computers
It's about time   we got hold of
some choice equipment.

we used to say   every ridge
don't spin webs   a bone
the white man says   every peak
don't spin wheels   a vertebrae
we turn that around   rising, forming
and say   to our   your skeleton
young   following every
spin creations   mound and crevasse
                                                     I see
                                                 your spirit
                                                   living

                                                standing upon
                                                  your skin
                                                   I feel
                                                 my spirit
                                                 living, too

That Dineh
man
he stumbled blinded
right across   the
Santa Fe Rail
looking   for the
curb   shop
in Gallop.
That white man shot him
said he thought   he
was   a   deer

Our mother is crying
Our grandfather
he looks at us
and he cries, too

I am a young woman
I respect my elders
I follow my heart
and   use my mind   to
benefit my community.
I am a single mother.
I respect my children.
I nurture their talents
and encourage   them to
use their minds
to benefit their community

The principals we were raised with
in a good way, as females, as
        Indians,
generosity; empathy; compassion;
loyalty...
                        Today
due to the monumentos
change inflicted upon us
by the European transplant society
marks us   like   targets
to be used, cruised, abused
conned and taken advantage of
even by   some of our
own   people

Continue on
on the other side
your walk
will be remembered
honored, respected.
Even   when   the endurance
is all winter   after   winter
all that really matters
is that you help
someone   somewhere
along   your   path
grow

Bull Bear
A warrior helps an old person,
a child, a single woman.
A warrior is not someone
with braids, sunglasses
and a cool statement

RLH
Phil Sheridan was
the hard enemy
he put the bounty
on the buffalo
Custer was nothing
but a rapist and baby killer

You better be careful
if you say the truth
the Feds will have
to kill you

They told us that

I wish I never told you
as much as I did
now you're a threat
you know too much

Defend your people
Defend our way of life
Be willing to give your life
to do these things

Physically, mentally,
emotionally, or spiritually,
even by laying
a hand on the shoulder
of a crying stranger
and praying in your
mind
You can help by
turning tears
to smiles and
laughter
if   the time
is right
grow
and help others
grow
and your tears
can also
turn to smiles
and laughter
rather than
falling rain
from the old
ones crying
above
continue on
this generation would
eat our children
What they meant
was that our men
would take our ADC
and drink it up and
for gas and leave
us and our kids
hungry and without.

One hundred thousand American
          Indians
reside in Los Angeles and greater
L.A. No greater concentration
in an urban community may be
found in the United States, even
          Almost
as large as the population on
the Dineh reservation (Navajos)

F.J. Thunder Hawk
For them only
They say it means
justice just-us

I went into the PHS in
Ventura County just next
door to L.A. and   there was
no box that said   American Indian
or Native American on the form.
        Once
again I checked off OTHER,
once again I got angry,
once again I understood,
this is our land, our health care
We are   yet   OTHER
only to you and
your voice of justice
The only forms I found
with a box   that identified
Native peoples   were
in Indian organization
offices,   where there were
no   other   choices
other than to modify   descriptives.
When   there is no   alternatives,
no choice,
modification   only is
offered, only modification
No solution No resolution
        Breaking waves
Thundering brain waves
pound in cranial capacities
and migraine me back home.

If   they truly respected
Crazy Horse they would
simply name a mountain
for him and leave the
physical form pure
rather than blasting
it into a replica
supposedly of him,
he who had no picture ever taken,
duplicating their idea of the
concepts he stood
for   and   gave his life
to   protect from
exploitation.

in 1492

Robert Grenier

Hot Afternoons Have Been in Bolinas

for Eli Siegel

Conditions are:

> — the 'weather' (November, the wind, the world itself —
> Martine — the name 'Martine', <u>green</u> <u>skin</u>, etc.)
> — the physical conditions ('soul-life') of the writer ('me') that day
> — <u>time</u> — literally 'having the time' revealed & possible
>   ('off-work') that day
> — who calls
> — will to deny all other 'influences' & side-track thoughts
>   <u>& </u>to include <u>same</u>
> — chalk & cliff (compatriots' & lizards' bones)
> — manifest shape-sounds (sound-shapes) —

The <u>world</u> is always, '<u>with</u> <u>us</u>' — 'here today'— can it be otherwise? — yes.

I am. (I exist as a 'no-man's land' <u>entirely</u> down at work.)

The thing is, to participate in anything '<u>like'</u> the (manifestation) agencies showing themselves <u>as</u> agencies —

> (or_____?)
> as Angels on the
> world's 'surface' in
> any moment that one
> lives & breathes &
> writes. The writing
> is nothing, is <u>as</u>
> nothing ('dust').

But to <u>seek</u> a various writing that participates in the world's agencies (<u>for</u> the writer) as the only 'reason' to be alive.

Take a 'season' (January), or a 'day' ("days, actually hours") — there's so much ( ) learning to be done to notice anything — what are the active, operable 'principals' given to me (the 'shapes') in language — how is <u>that</u> happening?

So you trace it, follow it, 'active it', become it in the <u>writing</u> itself (for the reader, too, words are nothing) — for the sake of being alive — that the wholly other may be here, as it always is here (irrespective, regardless).

And you imagine it.

The 'hope' (& <u>magic)</u> in language is '<u>here</u> <u>&</u> <u>hereafter'</u> — which is a living reader (could be the 'author') <u>alive</u> — as Walt Whitman knew — a leaf of grass —

myself —

— desire to "let Barry Sanders go about 100 yards"

— the 'mystery' is the 'form-factor', the 'combination' <u>with</u> whatever each is, now & forever !

Life, to live it <u>out</u> —

<u>How</u> is it always ('upbeat') feeling around, or form-forming ('whoo-whoo-ing') ? — structure of language (itself, of course, an organism — but '<u>not</u>') in proximity therewith — 'itself'? — ourselves, making what ??

Golden 'cup' o' the Moon setting into <u>(blue</u>-black sky) cypress grove —

Writing (making books) strange thing to be doing nowadays — the book is 'gone' as a form (trees are — who <u>could</u> make a book from trees?) (except myself!) — very few 'read' (each extant book is disappearing through use, or non-use, like a tree), etc. <u>Falls</u> <u>in</u> <u>woods</u>.

<u>And</u> <u>you</u> <u>imagine</u> <u>it</u> completely with the rthmms in words!

* * * * *

— r h y m m s, approx. 90 (8-1/2 x 11") — page green box (<u>boxes</u> are made, 'in substance '— about 500 of them currently exist, but <u>still</u> need interior hinges & some 'work' w/ green magic markers (keeping account of the making of <u>November Boughs</u> given in representative detail by Horace Traubel, <u>With</u> <u>Walt</u> <u>Whitman</u> <u>In Camden,</u> Vols. I & II, in mind))

— the first ones were <u>blue</u> (pens written w/ for years, not particularly 're-cognized' as 'color' <u>or</u> 'shape') — then <u>green</u> and <u>blue</u> <u>(</u>as <u>here</u>) — then <u>red, black, blue, green</u> (the very colors abroad in my 'workplace')

— NOW, <u>apparently</u>, four-color xerox at exorbitant rates w/ <u>really</u> poor colour reproduction (or color lithograph, in these <u>sub</u>-microscopic... — priced Out-a-Sight) Is No (Only) Way to call forth '<u>truth</u>' from my scriballings ('<u>copy</u> <u>it</u>') (meantime Bolinas photographer Ken Botto & I've made about 160 slides for record-keeping (& <u>to</u> <u>see</u>) from seven notebooks drawn between Sept. '89 & Sept. '92)

— WHO SHALL PAY to make the book 'primeval' ? — I will ! ('some day')

— Who <u>may</u> ("years hence") read it ? — YOU ! (just as anyone might today read <u>November</u> <u>Boughs</u>)   January 23/93

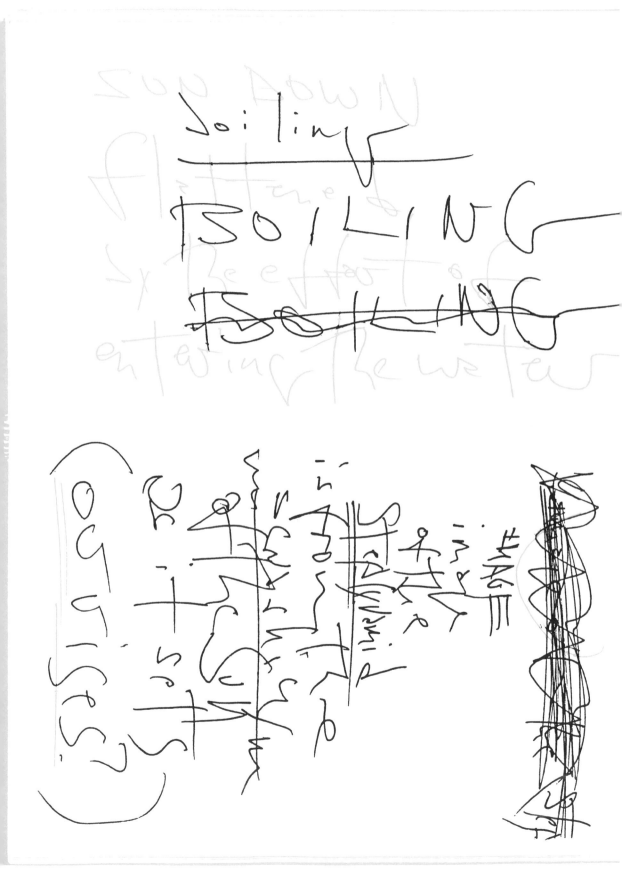

HUMMINGBIRD

humming birds

origination

SPIRIT LAKE

sewage pools

se I out over ...

Mess reflecting stve

WHAT?

forest to...

dying off

the World's f.sh

of half of ... imals

so the eyes +
ears link up
through peripheral
vision + in fact
only out of the
very sort of the
can't you see

RAIN FALLS ON

steadily in the

woods

rots it to the ground

phone the ground

fist that speech

RAIN FALLS ON

FOR Leslie

just as

a win

nothing.

write a 'rock' them

if you can

rock

Norma Cole

From: Rosetta

      went
his foot   down below the line
(the way) he painted blood
the blood
her name was on that place

word or name "It's not horrible enough

SPORTS   HARMONY
canceling, distant and hoarse draped
body the dancing uniform reverting "to nature"

§How should I read it revolves

§to break sense, host, hostage

the house: the building of the house
knocking at the door of its
habit of hearing providing context
completely filling in like a towel

as hesitation implies thought
so, they wouldn't cook

§nickname a sign of assemblage meant to uncoil

§moment into place unexpectedly convincing her

§no system in it

§no lucky winning system in it, nothing
that's not image, idea of

§sacrifice of the thing to it

                    non-regulatory
The Forests of Egypt
marked by this
(a life) by it   oneiric

worried that it wouldn't flush

            The animals were
                    punished
(is the story) "you will always
    look like this" witness the space
is full. so like them the
    little ORFEO

the color you expect is familiar

§*swell*
§could they both
have swallowed the same
sword or sun

§a new form of the letter: look for

§square of indivisibility, flowers

§growing out of his kidney "for epiphany" etc.
the wide changed color in the middle

            ...glass...
...smoked...resists this...

dream or long story after
my vigilance, my model
brief of long nights "love
erased imagined slights"

designated, marked for loading up "I placed"
the heard world's sheer relevance...the breaking
force...

    in rows in literal stone...stone inside the
neck...a curve of stone...
        ...tongue...

if the center of gravity shift
report to the light
a clearing. lying down in
rosemary. a quadrant. a
——lion rusting
of iron, of stone

§of shameless brass

§the rest is lost

§the rest is fact

    ...now...
or yes so...
    ...by the thousands

the disappearing type
...offers him to drink...
the direction of the will

to follow, or so to trace
with hands beams or grooves   *a guide of the*
region
~~invisi~~ble until they ink them

§in a vacuum

§elements of the false double door

§at the quai
    capucine
    nénuphar
    bruyère
    pensée

§Verona red wild chicory

...conducted peacefully...

        ...carved a menu for eternity...sacked
in an instant...the many parallel
grooves indicated fabric..."I decided to...
            I will drink"...

The inexorability begins   here.
under my sanction
wearing my coat
The two ways making that sound. the great ringed vessel
still unknown. the sounds were aground——our lips
are sealed against that formality representing their ideas
directly (the light of misfortune shines directly on you
la   rimavie

studded with...word...staging
...a sweetwater boat...

§material proposition of coexistence

§formwrecked

§narrow

§scale is ladder

§planted

§star is boxed

§a leg a spoon

§fog and thought are boxed

§going onto the rock

it may be the name of a queen
we are a sea going people
they have always been idealized
these letters "and trust to silence"
on the prow as an aside the hand
in a box

§refusal of light

I am epic, copying action,

weigh a fortune, to compete
in the sense of *fulfil* or *terminate*

shoe, recognition, then face
hair in profile, underwater
being carried along
by her shoe
by time or the size of
the stones
written in the shadow of
the ramparts
today we're dazzled by its absence
between time
or a dialogue

not just to understand the names, but to restore the page, letters filled with
plaster, partly effaced double syllables of affection sound a different word
for "bread"

... (the) blue next to the neck...
.......i........vo......tended and wild

§incorporating their measure

§comprehend as include

§the metaphor regarding someone speaking about you
  not in your presence

§your ears in the ground

§sunny side up

§or the palm game

Since it was a name, it had
no meaning. Names written on the ceiling
painted like a tent, words in front
repeated
reading monuments in the ground in the streets. The water
rises to the first landing every spring, flooding, like the
streets *as if there were time*

§startling from such a small

§bound in gatherings

(interior beyond imagination
        ....no contact.....
imperceptible) inner...
§where it says "work" or "earth"

HERE FELL

        the children were performing
        singing and performing. A bottle
        fell on stage, glass all over
        the stage, someone sweeping up,
        the children kept performing

Dear Scipio,
        I have seen your dream
on the wall......others have seen......
...memory itself...a new arena
put a roof on the old one, many......

no. no, Latin's latin. how
can it have accent, accident?
——-since the use

the point at which it is anchored

OPEN DITCH: Welcome to
Atomic City
      Agency X

(not yet) rules (?): we saw him (at first
just sounds) seated on the terrace

impulse to bridge

in the time of that
having been cut in half, how long
it (the scarf continued
to smell like her) of seeing
a place "that close"
"This is what we thought was happening."

Someone said, "It's a paradise," with surprise,
as though it had always been underestimated until then
or gone unnoticed dreams of bright blood red

§to do nothing

§in the small of the hands

§scratched "you're toast"

§   the missing
    were always missing

§only in the small muscles, if you
    know what I mean, in the little fingers

§sweet caps

§birds so bright you can
    read by them at night

the desirable qualities of distance
                the catalogue
of misrepresentations

"we played soft"

"we played pile"

        We played
the nature of that difference
    We played the music
underground.
a shape appears, the only given
or lateral action   on the small screen
red sail in play, the orders of inattention
the living frame, he opens the window
and someone reaches in, hands him a loaf

        S K E L E T O N A R Y
pinned to the wall the page
                maintains
            (for thanks for the book
now arrived now clearly
bound outlines the arrivals
outlives the animals
their modality...legible...
in relation to line, to mass
...*means*,

```
          cannot see well enough to
"at random"              (follow instructions
strange to    you

clearly



§added in

§from immediate

§working stone

§if you go into

§begging together

§is it history
   flowers tied to aqueous surface
   broke through the film of the
   eye well it's one two three
   who're we 'writin'' for

§one way street of course I'm
   prejudiced, etc....



§drawing the same proposal at the foot of the

§by then the margins have been resolved

§in full sail pass through the pillars



"true"
"original"
"copies"
syngyng
```

George Albon

From: Cosmophagy

The wheels of the jeep cut into the sand like a bite

and there were the outskirts those which only seemed not to be central to the di-
lemma's ever-widening contention-field fresh hollows somehow sprouting under
cover of equivocal daylight

and people had acceptable credentials for this line there was a clump of standees in
pessimal clothing on the periphery a hive of needs waiting to enter into the mouth
waiting to be fed

the convolutions meant to be there due to a belief in ongoing restlessness a plaintalk
nervation halfway up the meter and finally on the verge of showing through

a terrestrial image rising behind the heat wave and the skins inside the image
hooves moved slowly choosing the higher stones and thinner vistas as cardboard-
distance shifted in the wind

they had adopted a kind of sock that was rough against the ankles and calves they
could feel the surface in their feet feel as pain as the shoes refused to adjust to the
inside arch felt as a stated innovation

birds eat trees

part fell to the ground part the future nest length of note the short ones so many
against the long one more in a shaking list of projects in what looked to be forming
from vague material the year ahead

when the breeze stopped it started blowing different ways the steel arrows
spinning decisionless there was a leader but that turned into a rumor the film
started without warning or beep it was a line of soldiers and diffuse

a kind of pre-planned operative music swelling in the tracks where the feet land an
arrhythmic hand outside the screen patting-hitting the TV dots coagulated-
encamped on the lower-left-hand-side

weeping is for depending on state the new pastime or rather the old processes
brought forward through so many permutations that it has become the sense of
what to do an involuntary showing of colors

space after all signatures checked being covered seeing the wall while creeping
along it lift it higher he said lift it so you can clear the end of it world without
doubt the empty shout behind the eyes

life on razor walk as though parting intensity from its other half interesting grasses the sturdy reeds complicated centers there should be nothing that doesn't contribute that doesn't deny a growing denial

where can they go? the boundaries assumed till now not even up has the tonic resonance it had in past stairs only hinting at the vertical necessities the steps not planting the motion any way but sung

leaves pinnately compound and stay uprooted walking along with the dispatch if would could move the opposite way at an identical rate of speed it would demonstrate its willingness to be on the side of where the lights are turned

the lights blooming at night

what is history? or can anything be said to be in tune such incredible enmeshings amidst the giveless terms of the tall team such sturdy buds such drear colors as victory dogs follow in the wake exhilarated and gloating

Jerry Estrin
     from *Rome, A Mobile Home*

Brace

During the 1961 season, Roger Maris broke Babe Ruth's homerun record. At the conclusion of his final homerun, Maris cried: I've taken my last swing, I am finished. I will now be visible forever.

Diary: the grass on the field, the stands, heavy with fans, the press corp, high in the stands, and Maris, connecting with the pitch, the ball, soaring over the center field wall...

Maris, striking the ball, gives the homerun its form.

People running, the ball, invisible, in the single movement of the swing...

Perfection of the swing, white-out of the ball, a surfeit never extinguished, asymmetrical to the distant epiphany of its form.

Crowds intensely draw all stories to themselves, are capable of any form. Violence of the swing, then a roar.

Without inside, Maris, after his final hit, would not speak, or rather, there was the sight of his swing, caught on camera, repeating itself, forever.

Maris's swing, its constancy.

Night, Maris, under Yankee Stadium light, the crowd.

The crash of the ball, and Maris, caught in that instant, without inside, opening, to the evening.

Goodbye, he says through the night of the stadium air. Ah, I am finished.

Duration of the game, a player's ration.

Image of Maris, flap of pin stripes, under shadowless stadium light.

Image before, Maris at the plate, bat about to explode into ball.

The roar, the sound of bat on ball. The swing never post-game

but prior to definition, to description

to our agitation.

Repose, words of prose, existing once and for all, removed from bat and ball.

§

Lights of the far-off town
L.A. burning away.

On the far edge of the park
they shout U.S.A.! U.S.A.!

Now and before
the game returning to itself.

Wrong game.

§

Unflappable, unfathomed
Maris multiplies daily.

I go to the park, to watch the A's
make contact (the Oakland As).

A linedrive cannot help or hurt.
But a line from Zukofsky's *A23*?

He is where.

Death to the commissioner
when Maris kills the pitch.

§

Lebenswelt
The ball lost in the sun.

§

Maris

A spectral mosaic

Suffused by our thought of him

Whose swing divorced from anything

Roger, plaintiff of our autonomous community

§

In the major leagues

The ballpark lights go on and off

An impossible catch

A seventh inning stretch

Degù vous.

I mean what the stars have to sell is their autonomy

Maris, his oxengated simplicity.

§

Think of a film, an unmoving Roger Maris, whose doll eyes never flicker. Shot of the street, of rhythmical crowds, of Roger there.

Maris the modernist, sufficient to himself, has become the paradoxical hero of an instant that endures without a future.

Randall Potts

Abandon

for V.
Authority is to representation
as trauma is to dreams
Barrett Watten

I
Replicas wooden large
Low benches made for sleep
Stilled otherwise or obliterated as you know
Verb —leave hold of unclench quit one's hold foreswear
Abstain waste no time
Cataloguing roads alongside the trees
Thick green stench
Visible more as wreckage displaying this
To take our eyes off it
3. to yield (oneself) completely as to a feeling desire etc
Representing acquaintance with belief
Representing the other argument as in wide empty lawn
Not specifying color
SYN.—bliss rapture transport
Square filling the light
House compounding the dark
Everywhere this sense of the present we can't walk through
2. unrestrained freedom of activity
The gear turning his hand closeup
Syntax revealing it as ourselves
Tim conjugating the gaze for example
List in monuments enclosures
3. trance
A policy for grass for the watering and trimming of the trees
Verb—let oneself go riot go mad for joy

II
Fear naming names the secret was everywhere
A dark valley as equivalent you were in the foreground
To desire a whisper in color the background
Of any sort smeared being black or white
With our marks residue you were intermittent
Of sails smocks in the foreground but
Thin almost transparent in color the background
Almost desire leaves being black or white
Open in flames a slight indentation
One of us in color what do we do
In the foreground gold violet light burning
While the other is black in the sand what do we

Or white in the background do
To insist as if we were nearer objects often
All young at the same time partially occluding those
Filled not revealed further away
You are the same color spell copper-colored light
As the background at the outskirts
Which is black or white sweet smoke in our mouths
Consider the following by contrast well-meaning
Problem parallel line is a luxury we took to mean
And texture gradients took it for ourselves
Leading away from the observer to mean we were all young
You and I young in the same time
We could admire and the attached shadows
Be admired of objects changing
Ourselves meant to take with the visual
What we would field wide open spaces
Which was called desire where lines of thought
Thankless green day intersect roads elimination
A stone's throw away of dominated strategies
Waiting could be objects whose true size
A number is known wind finding
Becoming progressively the spaces filling them
Distance watch us mistake to approximate
Some remarks about relative to a still point
The definition perceived filled with belongings
Shapes cannot correspond the desire to fall
Each body alone in the clearing pierced
Of any foreclosing both of us in color
Trees in the foreground radiant
In reaching wind events bluish too slowly
Where lines of thought rubble stairs
Intersect roads what do we do
Light streaming amidst the approximate
From our mouths amidst the rupture
Pollen yellow trees this everyday life
Spell yellow alternating offers and
The smell of it one-sided asymmetric information
Wind described as everywhere this
Luminous forsaken body

III
Visualize abandon
Names naming fear
Everywhere the secret
Enormous viewing over range
Change that conditions

As described wind
This everywhere life everyday
Transparent almost here
Stairs rubble smoke
Transparent almost thin
Demands assemblage
Do what we do
Spaces wide open field
Foreground the us of one
Approximate to mistake
Around us turning time
Everywhere the secret
This everywhere life everyday

John D. Greb

UNEASINESS ALWAYS WALKS AWAY
Acoustic through guitar walls. Does she know? She must hint.
No. It is really up to me. Shyness flickers away
she walks. Words give strength. It is not even the
rejection. Slumber secludes races of two. To decline
an invitation not to be personal. Steam streaks
thoughts. To get past first visible verbal entrance.
To escape my own judgement of who I am. To divulge
my secrets is never the point. Secrets which are
merely nothing to hide.

Fingers drip warm Earl Gray honey. My breath licks the very bricks. The need so great that I smile in the dark so she cannot see. And as she approaches defences posture my own war. I become banal attentiveness. Uneasiness always walks away.

Eyes contact to movement without your blue. Your face I know.
You are like Boulder Creek Trout, yet invisible.
Oh, how I hate similes. Water bubbles my thoughts.
Courage spanks the past emerges. To go never forward.

WHISPERS STICK TO ME
Non-communicating finishing the point. Oxygen of my own betrayal. Sufficiently dry moon reads my hope. Hack my painting words are easy as it is walking. I had words once. They speak to me.

PARTIAL TRUE ACTS WOULD END CONFUSION

Faces story alive a consumption blends with specifics. No voice
    wire never my way. Super saturated somedays. My
    dimness self transient these words. Partial true
    acts would end confusion. This shyness is more of
    an obsession than you are. Troubadours if I can
    only sing. This is more than a whim looming. Aerial
    laughter skimps the white wall. Being alone gazes
    somewhere approximate the horizon, would be better
    with a hand.

CRACKING LEGS TOUCH THE EARTH

    The other distance wouldn't be here if apparent slamming lips. Flood light
the window. Cracking legs touch the earth. Dimensions shift proper progression
thought nights composed the unknown.

DEPICTING SOLUTIONS OF MY SHADOWS

Depicting solutions of my shadows. My foolishness is buzzing.
    Yes, I am hiding but I don't want to skip correct
    skidding further deeper arrived isolated to precision
    distance through fallen events, for only the purpose
    of by the wayside.

    Aggressive centuries handed down has bypassed me.

TREES MEAN I SIT UNDERNEATH THEM

    Connection of transparencies. Trees mean I sit underneath them. There are
no trees in the Lower East Side. The park is closed. Central Park is too far away.
Anyways, it is night, cold, and raining.

THE OPPOSITE OF BATTLE IS TO SPEAK

The opposite of battle is to speak. Repetition of thought
    since childhood. Where is the non-thought. Wanda tells me to
    come tonight and be strong. Strength is no problem
    if I get to know. Strength is always the after
    thought after parting. All I had to do was to
    ask if she wanted to go for coffee or a beer after
    the reading. My accusations of exploding self
    scratches the very known. I will want & wait the
    waves. Still trying to sense inwards that will
    never fit the tenor truth. Encounter the vanishing.

Exiting resonant retreats. Attach change to remove
the present and past.

RELATING TO SOCIAL AWKWARDNESS

Weightless hardness buries further. Relating to social awkwardness plots
my existence. Carrying on must cease escaping. If I am to clarify.

The argument of dislocations under questions that I don't
      have answers to. Charm is hideous if it is fake.
      Wit affirms the witness tug summers means being
      away if I picture too much.

      Inability eventually transform to new beginning. Why guard my skin? It
doesn't want it. History of walls...Light bearing the possible.

Flame, red wine bottle, opening contents memories arouse end
      if these times weighed.

MISPLACED TIMIDITY

Misplaced timidity.

I DO NOT STORM HER STATEMENT

Approaching. Approaching this to guilt. Through the television.
      answers appear but they are wrong. That is it guilt.
      Is that the right word, guilt? Is that the proper
      feeling? I am no better then those slimes that
      speech lies of motive to find gratis vacation of
      moisture. Is that important I ask myself—no & yes.

      Personal mitigation.

      Dealing with the indite past.

      Having extreme case of the hives from the unknown.

Stop to think of better incorporeal thoughts that remain move-
      ment. Someone said she wanted to sleep with me if
      I ask. Swooning chest swung the burnt star. I do
      not storm her statement. Walk off thoughts destroy-
      ed from my mind. No desire watching. If some other
      I would coast with music.

UNDERSTANDING THE UNRAVELING PREDATOR IN MYSELF

My metabolic latitude is dizzy. Consumed motion as evidence. Remember "The Master's" this afternoon and turkey soup alone. I could have seen her if I went outside. Maybe I'll go against my finances and go support my craving of beer and the potential that doesn't exist.

Personality of inarticulation.

I am going to retrace archetypal demolition. Emergence temporal stranger face. Understanding the unraveling predator in myself. Replace the unanswered edge by some other strewn kindle. Emphasis not as desperate. Struggle requested stricken century veins suffer these flowers overcoming desire. "Touching fierce exquisite flesh," she said to me. Do not bring in the past! Wakeful connection. To decide the concern. This sudden realm rubbing. Invite the seeking. Suddenly the tape ends. Storm madly adrifts. Omission of hesitation. Extending the contrast morning is losing astray. Particular shocking silent separate possible fluids. Stammering water. Collusion is the answer. Induced aquatic edge. Sensual plant light.

FENDING OFF TAR THAT IS WHAT IT FEELS LIKE

These bones. The pale soundtrack became angry. The restaurant
burst opened. The promise in the mirror is broken.
It is beyond a skim. This time and in most cases I
am deeper than non-chalance.
Where's the fucking dictionary!
The dissary of drying dishes. Was last night a
cleansing? The new birds of preception still can be
suspended and disturbing. A new disturbing.
Across the internal stunted expand.
Handling the motionless gradually mouths the hidden.
Scantily origin glowing gestures. Persistent photo-
graphic. The radio repeats existence.
Fending off tar that is what it feels like.
Magnifying the distinguishable self.
I cannot perform the silver wall.
Whirling tomorrow collides.
Opposite respective.
It wasn't meant to be screaming bottoms.

WHAT SHE DIDN'T UNDERSTAND IS THAT TECHNICAL MALFUNCTIONS CREATE NEW ART

Have I altered the story? My own place a blur camera. Emulative reflection. Swollen resistance.

Protective prop must be forgotten. Practicing stumble assur-
ance. I have to offer within myself first. Expand
the inhibition till it breaks.

This stupid hoax is really me! A life long cliche. Stumble sidewalks pass. What she didn't understand is that the technical malfunctions create new art.
Indefinite fault.
Touch loosens light.
What about the small edible town?
Illogical repellant bleed my persistent meanings =+ gestures.
Retreat is sublimation.
Joni Mitchell's "warm chord" slams the mention remembrance
       that is not aloud in here.

       Linear thought is incomprehensible that is why things are like this. This is why these words have thoughts that connect. Only because I say so.

Is this my novel?
Do you think she surmised my identity?
Without blankets time is dreaming.
I am losing energy that is why this wandering.
Should I forge further?

  SHE SAYS HE RUINS EVERYTHING EXCEPT SEX WHEN HE'S NOT DRUNK
To Denise's boyfriend, I am a friend with sexual qualifica-
       tions. Thus, a relationship of jealousy occurs.
       His friendless fences interferes. Empty weather
       savage. Angelic scrappings. Mutilated variance pub-
       lic tongue. She avoids my by way of embarrassment.
       Physical fallen dances. Transmitting trajectory
       extraction do not shape the horizon. Attempt tongue
       realizes her chin. A disgusting rejection. Saliva
       progresses the impossible edge glisten in smoke &
       light. Napkin pulls make-up away as she pushes him
       away.

       Saxicolous bastard, he burns a hole in my finger. I dump a beer on him. Tense astonishment with laughter. Michael rescues either of our first punches. She says he ruins everything except sex when he's not drunk. He is drunk. A sexual love. I tell her I like scars and I don't care about this disintegration but it eats me.

Fragmented forms remembrance.
Another guy is making a sex phone call on the public phone.
To another I'm trying to catch you, but I don't want to talk
to you.
The simple heart touches tenements.
Last night was a graduation.

PLANTONIC IS REAL AND CAN BE TRUE

With Denise sex is the furtherest thing. Plantonic is real
and can be true. Nothing more than freedom. Is this
a crumbling? Drop past energy. Surround the contempt
and shade the retreat. Response leaks salvation.
Anxiety thunder.

THIS IS THE MEANING OF SECURE

Someone said I am unreal. I have a hormonal inscription that balances equal. Respected tissue entrails. An unfinished destitute. Urgent gravity undercurrent fatigue me. Passive aggressive. Gradual motionless garden. Reveal motive of steam. Please generate your disappearance. My endeavors are pleasurable because I don't expect anything. That is why I am unreal.

Immovable relations are more important. Not saying a stag-
nated one but ones that fissure of individual think-
ing. This is the meaning of secure.

I have been told by too many ex-girlfriends that I am too nice. A sign of weakness? I am sorry if I can't pummel your face or force you to do things. If I did that that is not me. I am stronger than you will ever know.

ADVERTISE THE STREET WITHIN TO COMFORT THE PICTURE

New feelings appear without any occurrence. Disheveled help-
lessness is not the feeling but something more on
the outside of that. A sincere proportions erupt
shining. A control freak factor. This is what this
is all about, so vague declares.

Calibre the actual comradeship. Tolerate tension ambiguity maintains permissible acknowledgment. Soundness doesn't really want to know. Corpuscles enforcing reply. Projection represents the dominate edgement of response. Fuck disadvantage righteousness.

Well shocked honesty, that is the delicate pacifer. Accuracy
will never be the point of this. Tenacity maybe
something to do with absorption of conventional
distinctions.

Someone said she likes extreme impressions. Not talking to her is extreme.

Anyways, the afraid breath studys stain glass windows. Despite
my willingness to compromise I am an absolute body.

Writing wrist the throated light. Calmness form the inside must be broken barrier sighs. Palaces try not to decipher. Guilty struggle spending the creating. Historical is another book. Advertise the street within to comfort the picture. Maybe Bernadette is right I should never ask her out for this may cease. Well at least in this body.

Intelligent batters box. Dedicated to a problem. Particular
  substitution instinct. This is beyond an exercise
  the silence I live by. Suffer confidence. Comfort-
  able attendance controls courage. Sights drift
  over mollusks. My mind is drifting resources.

MAYBE IF OUR PARODY HAD GROWN LARGER

Last night, Gayle said, "You're more sexual than you come across." "I know. And was that an invitation? Not my place. Your place and only if you cognac." She did. I drank it all then left. I had no desire to sleep with her but I missed the morning with being with someone.

To arrive at a wish is never go into valleys.
  The thing that repelled me was her best feature,
  her eyes.
  Maybe if our parody had grown larger?
  Sensitivity submits notion. Yearning faulters inten-
  sity. We are better friends. Sexual indifference.
  Deemphasis respect is all that is left.
  The extreme is the only thing worthwhile—All else
  is fraud.
  I did notice the sky was sexual.
  The perfect equal does not live inside me. My equal
  is better than I. Me Me Me Me must quit the measure-
  ments.
  Seamless values is dropping a cool breeze.
  Grappling naked bodies damage the negatives.
  Sleeping with her or she me it wouldn't be a conquest
  for either side.
  If I've mistaken the oracle.
  Power opportune parables. Empty indication means
  all these words. The fact is water. The profit
  concaved. Picking the deflected indirection is
  what this and I am about.
  Simply to avoid.
  Gazed principles. Intimate eager strool. Familiar
  reactive prepositions.
  Volatile universe vanishes when certain tenderness
  taunts the border.

Concealing pervades the transparent.
Invisible avalanche. This is why we did not sleep
together because I could never attach myself to her.

I PREFER TO BE NAKED

It took me 2 1/2 years living with Lynn to learn how to match my clothes. So today people always comment how I appear. What they don't know is that over three-fourths of my clothes are from that relationship that ended over year and a half ago. Before that clothes were nothing more than a social obligation. I prefer to be naked.

Does apathy lead to being a good natured person? In my case yes. Good nature people have no opinions but people that have no opinions think too much. Somehow this leads me to decision making. I don't like making decisions, especially in relationships. It seems when I am involved with *thee other* they like me to decide on what to do, a father control factor. I always say I don't want to do that I will tell them. I guess they see that as a sign of weakness. My figuring is that if they decide on our plans is that they (we) will have a good time. For me, there is nothing worse than an unjustifiable nag. So I avoid all circumstances of ridiculous bickering. To tell you the truth it is really an act of selfishness. My selfishness is others happiness. So I thought. Plus, it allows me to think more about writing.

I'VE HAD THIS TINGLE COMBATIVE URGE LATELY

I've had this tingle combative urge lately. Actually more of
a rage that seeps through sometimes. A sick one
at that says John find a serious girlfriend.
Finding one isn't all that easy especially the way
I want it to happen. An instant explosion. 9 1/2 weeks
seems to be too tame to what I expect. I mean does
that really happen and last more than a week or at
most three months? But that is the way it's going to
happen. A stranger walking down the street.

I know that it exists. A recent conversation with Tara at Sophie's says she believes it. To her, I am the other but for me the explosion doesn't exist towards her. Mick tells me I should see her. I think he implies for sex or at least for companionship. He must be able to tell from my face that pre-dawn blue of the darkest blue mornings of waking alone are starting to get to me. I want more than sex. Which is amazing. My past has spoke against that but for the meanwhile one night of multi-heroic conquesting ejaculation isn't for me. In the end I would break her heart, I would fall in love with her but that burning obsession would falter, or, worse yet, I fall in love with her and she dumps me. A coward.

A FEMALE STUCK IN MY WHOLENESS

The harbor of silence. Language not submissive to desire.
Mutilated picking the conditions. Violent lesion
weather sweeping. Direction of the happening, a
mechanics shadow. Detaching the sky of misunder-
standing. Replacing behavior of monotony. A parti-
cular landscape illness. A blink occasion. To treat
the function of crying. Orphaned rain. The reference
within the truth, a frenetic mirage. Severe rain-
bow ceasing with me. Saying through eyes that fits
the light. Caress of emptiness beguiling. A sudden
frequencies of nakedness approaching language.
Rocks breathe confusion. Revoke puddles of luminous
spasms. The occupied parameters of nowhere. A fe-
male stuck in my wholeness. Crazy blue entire sucks
my alarmed content. The context of craddled fields
of absence. Slowing the articulate wound. Pushing
the grandiose adjective of communicated proba-
bilities in gravity hope. Idling the averted fore-
ground. Ink penetrates the satisfaction. The danger
of disposition turning the concern. Instant appli-
cation emerges. Swelled ephemeral strengthen
unbottom hills.

CURSED REASONS OF ERROR SALT THE EROSION THAT CANNOT ALWAYS LEARN IN THE SENSE OF UNDERSTANDING

Thrown from seeing the revoke. The impossible definition of an edge of a puddle that soaks a sponge. Traces of ink bloat the shadows horizon of unbroken subtle rising satisfaction. Only if the source of water is frantic rain of fact. My leng- thened zone bracelets the energies of swelled seasons.

Opaque of difficulty. The dial disappears the attachment. My
specks of periphery hipped the reason of the outlined
clarity and confidence. The previous language repeats
the untangible that repeats the purpose of a promise
that traveled hours of absent posture.

Lack of a neutral among the stillness outweighs the patches of absent silence. Anxiety engages the width of an advancing blur. I must consider the cutting of uncertainty with her mirror of useless compass. The distance needs an explana- tion of reflective blue weight. To tell her the strangling motion. Transparency posses the incompetent friction. The vacancy is naked, through her postulates desire. Correspondence of the empty piano that disappears the writing. The fishline rejection that passes the constrict beginning of the street. Metaphor dims the impression of linear anatomy. Cursed reasons of error salt the erosion that cannot always learn in the sense of understanding. Diagonally reaching peculiar darkness adheres to grammatical sidewalks of broken glass. The phantom drums the bottle.

TOGETHER OF A BRIGHT PARKING BETWEEN THE KNOTTING AND NARROWING OF YOUR TIME IN HISTORY

Your complicated investment ignites slippage from merging
        gentle noises. Mysterious rhythm sighs. Hanging your
        clothes up would only misunderstand the eagle sing-
        ular sound of our flight. Dimensions of depth the
        exaggerated theology is not all that heroic within
        my emptiness, this I said to her. The reverse of
        language and body towards navigational driftwood
        and still hunger the string pictures of our sea
        vanishing. Never touching thickens the sex. Sharp
        definition flattening the boundary of the gaze.
        Private promise that won't resemble the fused thought
        that grasses the twisting demands of me holding the
        ledge from the shadow of your legs. Why do I
        desert the resemblance that allows the hydrants
        remarks? Together of a bright phrase parking between
        the knotting and narrowing of your time in history.
        The indifferent of infinity. Resonance substance
        repeating the mystery of me not speaking my constant
        thought. Androgynous. Ungraspable horizon points
        through splashing bodies.

Resemblance in location of empty syllables that hinge my detachment that is falling in useless crowding. The ungraspable solution protects the excitement dominates the bending rekindle propensity of your gesturing body. Narrow through the excepted wet. Maybe a fainting street in rain the appearance of a kiss. The strange mountain side of legs linger. Doctrine rapture clashes. Our bouquet museums breezes as whispers. The defiance of the flower haze entered. Defeat of passing birth. Investive of abandoned promise. Epiphany. Telescopic depth observes fierce delicate attentiveness becomes our ocean of early dawn habits. The guitar dissolves which at once an hour ago soothed our beginning now in half wish of a dream fell away without concern. You, I reach the edge that reminds me of a terrain of voices, a peculiar sunset. The infused contingent ignites the edge of our incursion. Burning emigrants reflection. Sighs & Screams the circular and the coastal.

In the middle of the dawn you leave without warning, never to
        be seen again, two days after...

THE ARGUMENT SENTENCES THE LONELIER RECTANGLE OF THIS BUILDING

Understanding the sound that landed daylight. The argument
    of the landlord thighed the seeds. The children of
    hydrants skin countries, besides the solidity of
    gloves.

Apart from the ocean the river chews my sleep.

The condition wants a green plunge.

Yes, last night trilogy of chicory waves describes corpuscles pauses my guilty heroic inflection. Listening through the mural apart for similarity of the white that decides the thawed beauty. The movement of sticking space. Texture real beauty acted upon in footprint in happening. The argument sentences the lonelier rectangle of this building. The outline of his mustache of anger that address his doubts. The listener addresses through the sedative mention of skinned civilization.

It is we as individuals that must seek deep within our own
    soul to know, find, solve the forgotten frame of
    humanity. Thus, it is then we can see into history
    and with that history the knowledge of change can
    exist.

We the individual, as today, must be history, beyond the history that we perceive day to day, and take away the history that is handed to us.

We grow we grow...At times destruction is the only way to
    see failure.

I BREAK HIS CHARACTER FOR A MOMENT

The muscle of water sprays against the building disregarding other's moments in music. The Con Edison man washes away what he is told. He also thinks the posters are disrespectful. He washes my beauty away. I break his character for a moment. He tells me to "Fuck-Off Asshole!" I smile in his face and walk on.

SIRENS AS THE NEXT BREATH

Children leave during stages of dark. Through the street this
    town sleeps my light. "Why do our legs sweat like
    the dew at dark? Like a vase? Mystery of child birth.
    Grave visitation. What is it that calls us? Why must
    we pray screaming? Why must not death be redefine?

We shut our eyes, arms stretched out, whirling on a
pane of glass. Infixation. Fix on anything. Line
of life. The limp tree. The hands of he. The promise
that she is blessed among women."

Among the dandelions, new robins, a place where direct sunlight never hits,
my future holding...Vague New York as I sit across the grass. Poverty has never hit
me harder. Fire hydrants filling plastic jugs. Vicinities meeting the weight of eco-
nomics. Rotting vegetables in the grocery store. Sirens as the backbone of breath. Si-
rens as the next breath.

Carla Harryman and Lyn Hejinian

A Comment on The Wide Road for O

Five years ago, in the course of a casual conversation, we found ourselves
agreeing that, because language is active, anything in language could be
erotically charged. Because we have both had a long term interest in "land-
scape," (construed as history, milieu, etc.), we decided to depart as collabo-
rators from "a broken house" and venture out toward a horizon of "measured
desire." Taking with us from the "broken house" the copy of Basho's *Narrow
Road to the North* which happened to be sitting on the table, we used it as our
initial guide to style. The casual shifting between poetry and prose provided
us with rhythm for our erotic exploits, and the geographical fluidity of the
picaresque genre provided us with a necessary narrative mobility.

We were "we," meanwhile, for several reasons. First, it allowed us to
have more than the usual number of body parts. Second, we were determined
to adventure across normal boundaries, or to blur them at the very least. The
identification as "we" allowed us easily to include each other in the work all
the time and to identify with each other continuously. This provided us with
unusual liberty and power.

Often, if not always, the quality of being "we" has been more impor-
tant than gender. The body with *its* knowledge, as distinct from knowledge of
the body (language), is not gendered in its thought, though the body can be an
instrument for celebrating the power of being gendered. Paradoxically, the act
of writing can be similarly unbinding. And writing as "we," we are able to
embody/sex even more than we might if we were only travelling through a
land of singularly defined difference.

Sex is about difference—about experiencing, contradicting, and crossing
distinctions. And there are ways of crossing distinctions which may or may not
involve sex but which create a liberated space through the blurring of identi-
ty — a blurring which collaboration emphasizes. Certainly there have been
other collaborations that have achieved the kind of liberation we enjoy in ours

— John Ashbery and James Schuyler's *Nest of Ninnies* and Andre Bréton and Philippe Soupault's *Les Champ Magnétique* among them.

In recent years, the generative possibilities of the erotic imagination have been less often documented than the limitations of the alterity involved. In our work, we have chosen to subvert the rigidities of identity rather than explore (á là *Thelma and Louise*) either the limitations or the complexities of socially stagnant roles.

That we haven't identified women's pleasure in heterosexual sex with a particular age group or a particular problem seems to have stimulated many of our readers.

                    our hum off a stiff horizon
                    a captain came with a can of nuts
                    his wet ship was in

                    its high fleas are fish
                    one flea reached the end of a pubic hair

We thought the flea would belt us or scream, "You can't have him, he's mine!" We thought this because we'd been reading fables while watching TV in the fog. But then we realized for a second time that the flea was a fish, and its attraction to the crease between our legs was obvious.

                    truly the legs are used
                     in fog differently

we wrote on the side of the ship. The captain sent us the following response in a bottle filled with court bouillon:

                    drink the fog differently
                    sweeten the drifting leg's anchorage

We responded from the nether part of the ship:

                    the drink tests sheathed vegetation
                    but what if greens only require a trickle?

Our robe fell off our shoulder while we awaited the next response. Its coarse material excited our already throbbing bulbous breasts. Any minute our fleshy legs smeared with court bouillon would turn to foam. What was keeping the captain? Anxiously we sat on our hand. A tickle crept down the inside of our thigh. It was the fish wiggling out of its hiding place. In surprise we moaned, "Oh." The next thing we knew an enormous breast had lodged itself in our mouth.

Simultaneously a hat fell on our foot. We could barely see it or feel anything except the court bouillon smeared all over us bulging with zeroes, all of them as soft as fawns' muzzles. Our head had been forced against the back of the bench by the mouthful of breast. We sucked voraciously and opened our legs as wide as we could to accommodate as many zeroes as possible. Our hand groped around on our thighs for the fish.

The captain laughed a feminine belly laugh. "You'll have to search my pockets for the fish." We were not timid. Our hands slipped into her tight little back pockets, which on the inside were punctured and full of holes. Little rounds of flesh were revealed to our finger tips. Cramped inside though they were, our fingers tore at the material, enlarging the holes until the inside of the pocket had been entirely ripped away. Our hands grabbed around each moon of ass. But our fingers, when they reached for that warm tunnel between moons, could not get there. We pulled them, cramping, out.

The retrieval of our hand from the dark caused, or seemed to have caused, the captain to jerk up and dislodge her breast from our mouth. We were a bit relieved, since it too was beginning to ache. "I need a break," she said and sat down, abruptly, next to us. Where just a minute before we had only a view of flesh and sky, we now had a view of a sailor standing next to a thick hose. But before we could remark on this, we realized that the captain had unbuttoned her pants and that she had placed her hand casually on her cunt mound. We were going crazy and jotted the following message on an old fig leaf we kept around for emergencies:

> We thought you'd be a man with
> a can of nuts drifting in the fog.
> Now the fog is fully fog. And we
> are fully anchored here. Your ship
> has joined us, too. But where
> is the can of nuts?

We read the note to her since she seemed unwilling to take it. As we spoke the word "nuts" she gave her clit a little pinch and gave way to what appeared to be an orgasm of great magnitude, which lifted her arching right up into the air and flipped her overboard. We ran to the side of the boat just in time to witness an enormous translucent fish tail disappear into the water.

We were now bent over the side of the boat looking a little sadly at the water. Its green fingers slapped the boat with a near lethargic desire. How were we to relieve ourselves of this overpopulation of zeroes pressing in at our thighs and filling up all our nether parts?

> Let us go lie
> under a waterfall

We walked inland for about 15 minutes until we heard the gushing sound we had been hoping for. When we arrived at the site of the falls just over the shrubby hill from where their sound first reached us, we found the sailor, who had been watching us on deck, fully undressed, lying on a slippery rock right under the smallest of the waterfalls.

The water was striking him, directly but gently it seemed, and he had an enormous erection. We trembled with erotic emotion and let our robe slide away from our body. We mounted and slid around him. Water fell on our back and ass like a torrent of desiring hands and flapping fish. As we slid very slowly down on him, filling ourself with him, the zeroes began to pour sweetly out of us into the water, filling the water with our ohs and our ecstasy.

Filling the water with our sleep.

Sleep was now rolling in a little stream and we lay at the edge of it. We tasted it with the tip of our tongue. The sailor moaned.

"You will never embarrass me," we said.

Sleep always contains a little milk.

Heraclitus said, "Those who are awake have one and the same world in common; in sleep each one returns to his or her own world."

Being completely alone means, psychologically speaking, dreaming.

To dream means: I don't know what is happening to me.

We snuggled with the sailor beside the water, watching the water perpetually divide and repeat. Occasionally we sipped — the water was always ready. Several hours went by but they were difficult to perceive.

"What never leaves can never stay," the sailor said.

Soon the shadow of the evening sun was turning the water red, and the sailor put his pants back on.

> blind as milk
> but your hands full
> no seabirds can tell
> of our breasts as we blow

One night in the bar we were sitting with a man who was drinking coffee. "The sea is not amorphous," he said, "I know this because I'm a captain. It is not a container, either. But if you know what you're doing you can fish with success. The sea, by the way," he added, "is not like music either."

"Our mother always said," we said, "that comparisons are odious. She was talking about Mrs. Mortar, a neighbor mother, who was always comparing her son Johnny Mortar to our temperamental brother. But we can see how what she said might have something to do with the sea."

The memory of Johnny Mortar and his mother, Midge Mortar, had come to mind very suddenly, and we remembered the smell of their dachshund on rainy days when Mrs. Mortar would persuade us to come over for cookies and then tie us to the chair and tickle us.

"Is remembering at all like fishing," we asked, leading up to something.

"I'll let you compare them for yourself," the captain said.

Already this is endless.

        beauty floating beauty floating
        the surface of the sleep is roaring

    We discovered that remembering is not like fishing, any more than
forgetting is like fucking. Mama was right that comparisons put someone at a
disadvantage, and this someone is often someone's brother. The overlapping of
things at sea and the movement of things within often make people's brothers
nauseous, but we enjoyed it immensely. The captain laughed, then asked us to
cook some rice and spice it with pickles, declaring that we were certainly nobody's
brother.
    "That's a sexist request," we said.
    This provoked a big amorous response. But things on deck were busy, the
fishing boat was bouncing, the fish were coming in, and the captain was suddenly
blushing. "I apologize," he said. "Really."

    We softened.

        thousands of smudges
        not all from memory
        what else occurs in a flash

        ice
        winter
        ice
        or
        not
        smudged
        city ice

        the wall falls and floods
        the tongue
        on
        the roof
        is gritty
        and jelly

        a steaming wall among feet

        just under
        the tech
        a hand
        pelts
        rains
        parts

        within broken synonyms

I
me
you
they
us
and
she
he

Those were some of the smudges organized on the smudged surfaces, folded inside some memories, which were in turn entwined in comforting habits of organization while the wars met on each side of their beginnings and endings.

And people follow wars — certain people, titillated by the almost medically sanctified certainly medically ritualized televised preparations until half of them long to plunge their self-righteousness into a grand allegiance and the other half is frenzied with a desire to receive and solace the resulting force.

"I've such a crush on The Blackhead," said a certain Margaret Format, whom we met at one of the popular television cafes in the town of Rocky Welf where the fishing boat had put in. Civilians in camouflage shirts unbuttoned to their navels circulated among the clientele. "Do you want company?" one would ask the girls. "Or for extra money I'll put my big gun down where you can feel it." One such civilian took a pose at our table, hands on his hips, legs spread so his balls hung down from the slit in his pants. But Margaret Format began to coo: The Blackhead was slowly unbuckling his belt; he did it with one hand, while he rumpled his brushcut with the other. "Oooo," said Margaret Format, putting her hands over her breasts and squeezing them. "He's so cute." The Blackhead let the ends of his stiff leather belt drop and swing. Then he turned and as his pants dropped he mooned. "Oh, god, over the desert! It's gorgeous. It's too much," said Margaret Format. "I can hardly breath, I've got to see a Bud ad, a cold Bud for my cunt." Instead The Blackhead's striptease was interrupted by the familiar neon display of the names of the dead. "Thank heavens," said Margaret Format — "I don't want to come before total victory."

sacrifice
paradise
scrape the pudding
liberalize

make the gutting
more and moralize

ape the studding
appetize
infantilize

The Blackhead was back on screen and Margaret Format stared at him. He was naked, holding a pointer in one hand. He touched the pointer to a map. "This is a member nation," he said in a low emotional voice. Reverently he looked down and began to stroke his glowing oiled penis. "Oh, no," moaned Margaret Format, "war is too cruel, oh no, I'm . . . I'm . ."— she had spread her legs and was gaping at the television ". . . oh . . ."she was pulling at her panties —"War is hell!" she moaned. "Oh," she screamed, "No! . . . I'm eviscerated."

We had come into the tv cafe at Rocky Welf exhausted after a night and day at sea, and Margaret Format's collapse was so final that, though everything preceding it seemed prolonged, when we were called into the police station to describe what had happened we could hardly explain. The cop showed us a photo of Margaret on the autopsy table. Peace had transformed her agitation. Her eyes were closed, nothing needed to be expressed. Only the handle of the pair of scissors that had been stabbed into her neck was visible.

The contrast between the violence of her death and the tranquillity of the photo was almost religious.

We vomited.

We were excused.

We left Rocky Welf in a rented two-door car.

　　　a clue is only a buttonhole
　　　the button in turn is cajoled
　　　o man(sic)kind, get wide

A red tulip the size of a dinner plate with a scent is for sale. We pull up to the nursery in our rented car.

"We haven't received our bulbs yet, but I know nothing of the tulip you speak of," says the gardener.

There is something peculiar about the nursery. It seems unremittingly sexual. We conclude we have never seen a flower until this moment. It is as if each plant opens and closes for us. Why did they have a life of their own before? And the speckled perky plants hugging the ground appear to be backing away from us. We are a sexual monster spilling our eyes onto their tiny throats.

Some flowers bow their heads in longing. We are thinking particularly about a modest star-like gladiola, a single flower bent at the tip of an emerald stem. Clearly it silently hungers to brush its face against our open hands.

　　　It longs
　　　to handle
　　　our commands
　　　with soft ears
　　　dancing around
　　　sword spinning fins

This great pleasure in power pollinates our face until it seems as large as a dinner plate. We cup our blooming nose (our Nose of Sharon), smack our over-hydrated lips, pinch our mud-leached eyes. Our legs are twined with passion vines. Their whirligig blossoms sip our cunt juices and quietly pilot themselves into cup and saucer emptiness. A monstrous swamp gut power pours out of us. With our entrails inside out and outside in and in and in, we stand on our bolas, wondering how in Ovid's name we got here.

> But the plate
> the lips
> the tulips
> and a kiss
> were meant
> for undermining
> the duplicitous
> state

"We got here through the rear," we said laughingly to the inquiring rose who then remarked, disdainfully, that she kept as far away from swamps as possible, and since she couldn't move herself, perhaps we could remove ourself to the lily pond where she was sure the dragonflies were dying to meet us.

"Yes, fine, we're on our way," we said, "but can you just tell us one thing, do any of the dragonflies go by either the name of Donald Duck or Schwarzkopf?"

Her leaves paled to a vomity green. Rust inched its way up the tips. Her head dropped over and the petals dropped off instantly. Yet, even without her persona, her thorns glistened and raised the hackles of the surrounding foliage.

> Yes, they were shouting
> penstemon
> of the bearded tongue
> as if this were the key
> to Schwarzkopf

Suddenly, an idea grew on us. Our limbs spread. Our sexual orifices filled with birds of paradise and sprays of daisies. "Is there a variety," we ask, "that has black heads and a bearded tongue? Is there someplace they grow in profusion? And what happens if we pluck them?"

Aching with knowledge, like dirt farmers on dark ground, we know that plucking is never final. We are in a transitional zone here, unpossessed and unpossessing.

There are certain places — inhabited sites, populated locations — that can be mobilized, transported in lives, and reestablished — Italy to Little Italy, Russia to Little Russia — but empty places remain where they are. Wyoming, for example, can't be moved. And it's a place where it's hard to garden.

But we arouse flowers.

"What you pluck here is bound to disappear", as they say on the occasional morbid billboard that has escaped the ecological knight known as the Green Fox. His motto, rumored but nowhere inscribed, was "Set Undeclared Precedents."

We could see this would lead to cycles.

We know cycles. We also know ripples and topples. Each in its place, we say.

We have romantic and real desires. These are logical eroticisms.

We can merge more than we already have.

> a saturating thought
> of shadows

We like to have sex outdoors in the sun where the sun can see into our pants. We pull ourselves a little open. This feels a little daring, a little un-abashed, a little fertile, and it's all of these. The sunlight begins to focus on us, the colors swirl and converge, the heat on us increases, even burns slightly between our legs, as the sun looks in.

The sun can't measure.

Lori Lubeski

From: Sweet land of (fabric) woven

When one is so far and unreachable
distance holds extreme beauty

wings that describe

she in her own mind (element)
standing above ground

feeling the plates under her begin to shift
(starts to pull)

§

Like a cemetary whose bodies glow (aroused), intrepid,
destined even to warehouse glass. Behind the fire a small
caged animal

§

Such life force measures.
Plates crashing up against each other
like cracked vertabrae without a disc
to buffer the friction. To be taken as a
landowner when in fact you are only
a slave to the elements

§

When one is nervous, more importantly illusive,
dine alone beneath table while sections of continents
ride up over each other in concise descriptive movements
while under gloved hands one remains alone,
a fraction of the small world which has loved itself
continues to (rocky assault) touch the other parts.
However skeptical this belief in theory draws she alone
the ambiguity of plate tectonics while on her way
the ground in waves
releases such pressure

§

No world drifts theory
voices elapse from a strong boyhood dream

§

Another dark night begins to impress its structure
on your rich and growing earth. This country's westward
motion has wiped out part of your love for the Pacific Rise.
Tomorrow you will have awakened to solidification against my face,
ribs, and backbone glamor of the only necessary trust

§

From the shallower areas you pull
part of the words (sandslide)
from his world version and memory
transgresses soft bodies to reveal
viscera, verbal eyes, a traditional
flaw in your method of explanation

§

Your car moves across the desert like a man in the mojave
Sanskirt elbows worn envies, (obeys) desires put forth
by moving juxtaposition of one trench subducted by
deeper spreading

§

Memory returns to natural wonders
so frequently urge to get home-
fallen forgotten latitude (watermark)
on a ship's bow. Oh, incomplete rage of
the hottest zone

§

The long hallway toward home,
isolation's individual crack of lips
against the seal of an envelope.
Light crystallizes into belief
and from the corner of your eye
you begin to see translations,
magnetic reversals of the long hallway in

§

When the moon locks gravity into place,
your body, tides and subcultures. Only at
ground zero are we able to express ourselves
(freely)

§

You call me from far away
when I am remembering ideas
of subduction and love returns
with memory plagued by definition.
The divine urgency parallels the
(glossy mouth) repulsion

§

With one wing in the (lithosphere floating)
a melancholy body attracts a mood which floats
upon the earth's mantle. Below his feet crowd
the movement when shelter feels so elusive,
home, a melancholy body far off

§

In glass light the would-be sun still looms.
Preservation of a world in bodies, converging
epicenter of difficulty. The bloodhound eyes
inset a criminal mind forever the capillary
of intimacy like sweat coats the skin
of constantly grating edges

§

Voices still hoarse
from treasured (pale)
rides on the skin

§

I've returned, shifting the plates
under my ground

as sea level rises
and within hours
this tectonic rush begins.

To say the word, "brother",
you remember linguistics carefully

it is no rumor which scares you (bread alone)
the criminal in this darkest moment
in front of a small house interrupts
your sequence of events

Home feels so (distance) against your side
or as in figure eights as one skater
around the rink (world) shifts

§

As in music, continents against each other slash-
the tectonic theory amuses even the most criminal mind.
Her eyes in blue, a small figurine reaches toward longing
plates (friction) or buckle which causes pressure, harmonic,
to build, requires the space of a dream

§

With the word (brother) remains a category of forgotten landscape.
Crushing plates force a body out of a mouth, whereas forgiveness (criminal)
interferes with the structural deformation of thought. When one is far away,
a tectonic balance cannot be attained. In building a relationship, small home
feels even more distant than wet tongues over a forbidden area (ice).
The strain of geology on description which floats (is floating meanwhile)
on a thin layer of air

§

Surgical belief in routine (tiny route) home.
Mummification of a corpse (fissure), stagnant
humiliation of a wet body clothed dampens burial.
Warm preservation of an indian rain

§

Songs that were sung in order of learning.
Majestic equivalences of patriotism.
My country (Mediterranean Sea) gasps
in catastrophe. You were too young then, you're
only six, brackish water seems unthreatening,
clouds cover the darkest sixes; murky lakes of
the Persian Gulf personified

§

Ceylon poisoning and beach days subsequently
imagine trinities of fire and your watery eyes
give birth to transgression. Home, that ivory
parkway just past high tide shows traces of
missile paths, airplane wings diving. Oh,
justified few who believe in your country
(tis of thee)

§

Sweet land of (fabric) woven.

Milton Apache

CABAL DEVOURS KISSES

Night falls followed by day break.
While Springtime calls for the rain washed valleys.
and for the butterfly passing through windows and
gardens furnished with mahogany trees.
Apple orchards turn from a plum purple to
a blossomed pink, trimmed with white edges.

A woman has been seated, and her son is walking through the garden.
He crosses a little stream, and heads toward the apple orchard.
Suddenly, she announces that he should not be there.
But it's too late, the thorns of the nearby cactus,
grabs the boy on the legs, torso, and arm.

The woman can't get up to save the boy, because
her tongue is caught between her teeth.
She can't open her mouth to scream, if she does
a spider will make a web between her opened mouth.
allowing the butterfly to become caught.
The boy moves, but the thorns stake their claim
into the boys blood soaked leg.
He yells hoping for some assistance.

But howling wolves drown his plea for help.
They are feasting on a butterfly, that has
landed on an iris petal to rest. sharp teeth
crawl into the butterfly's head and side.
As the butterfly becomes devoured the pack of wolves lay
on the grass and stare hungrily at the boy who is now frightened

A circular wave of motion, intertwine hands   a right and a left
This reminds the boy of butterflies, weaving into Lilac bushes
The only thing that remains now, are the pungent smell of the
of the purple flowers.

Trying to escape, the cactus clings to the boy even harder
The boy screams, just as he remembers the woman
laying on the ground.

Across the stream, the spiders web
recovers the butterfly that had his leg caught, but
through his struggle the butterfly relapses, only to become restrained..
The woman is facing upward, to the boy it means nothing.

Jesus come down, you're the only one who seems to care.

Howling wolves cry in the distance. Over the moors, beyond the countryside., (lay) between two ridges..

The indigo skyline
brushes against the mountains. The mahoganies and apple trees
lose their brilliance, and flowers lose their prism glow.
The spectrum of rays decease to a cold grey.

Eileen Myles

THE POET IN THE WORLD

I was at McDowell a couple of summers ago — there was a poet there whom I knew, somebody whose work has nothing to do with mine, we know each other for social reasons, because we're both gay. There's a lot of that in New York. You can know all sorts of people. Anyhow I was sitting at the dinner table with this guy whom I know and he says "Eileen where did you come from"

> I did spit out an answer
> but what it brought into
> question
>
> why was I at McDowell
> did I belong at McDowell
> Where is it that a poet "like me"
> should be & it brought up
> the whole question
> of how a poet exists
> in the world & where
> does she belong &
> where does she want to be.
>
> There was a little titillation
> about "getting into"
> McDowell
> but chiefly it was economic
> if I could get in
> it was free
> unlike a month in a third
> world country
> or a month in a house

simply to write
I realize I have a complete inability
& a desire
& a complete discomfort
at the idea of
"going away to write"

I write "in" the world
that has always been
how I see myself as a writer

it's ironic
I spent the first 24 years of
my life arriving at a
point where I could
give myself permission
to do this thing
that has to do
with interiority
& have spent much
of my time
since then
trying to establish
myself as an extrovert
in that community
of introverts
and even
see the poet take
her place among
the community of artists
or even a world
of "doers"
people with jobs
a function in the
world that everyone
knows about

So I see myself as a poet as pretty janus-headed and I'm feeling prescriptive today so I'm saying that I know what I want the poet in America or even, certainly, in the world to be. I want the poet to be of use, to be visible, to have a body and a voice in the world of power & politics.

As I approach and use that word voice all that janus-headedness I mentioned becomes abundantly clear because of course a voice has a body & a mind & rattles your soul & gets heard on the street, is how you got called home in all kinds of light.

In Leni Riefenstahl's movie *The Triumph of the Will* , Hitler, the physical monument of the man, Hitler, is established cinematically as he stands in a motorcade through arches, light & shadow, like I said about the voice in all kinds of light and it persists he is truly a man who never changes, is able to lead.

I think the voice is a similar though more wriggly kind of embodiment. Always the same, your mother's voice, your lover's voice — as utterly recognizable as a gait. I mean I think it's a falsehood that Hitler never changed, it was the essence of the lie of fascism that one human could be the same for everyone & that that could be good.

The human voice must be chemical, right. I am approximately five feet six inches tall of Irish & Polish extraction, female, catholic upbringing. I am forty-two years old. My parents were workers. My father was a mailman, mother a secretary in a toystore. In Massachusetts. The last time I went to confession I confessed that I had committed impure acts. In a confessional you kneel in a dark musty place and you speak to an invisible man through a bit of scrim. I told him I had committed impure acts. He asked, "With another boy?" In many ways I am still living in that stunned silence. Then I'm I'm I'm a girl. My status as female is unsure. I carry this ambiguity in my voice. In the early '80s when my alcoholism required that I only do job hunting from bed I frequently worked in telephone sales. I'd find an ad in the *Voice* call up, they'd see that you could talk and you were hired. At work I proceeded through the confessional veil. I felt great ease on the phone. I was very successful. I had the ideal businesswoman's voice. I was told. I think it's mannish.

I think the voice is a kind of soup or a weather. You look up at the day & you see the tone of the sky. It's resonance. We are all sort of swimming in the day, surrounded by it, that's why I think of it as soup. When I was an active alcoholic the hangover, this is almost too difficult to speak of but there is a connection so I will go on — the hangover, a form of psychic poisoning, was like a low horizon in the day under which I would make a lot of poems as if the day ended early or hadn't started yet, there was this artificial line, this tremulousness of body & mind a synthetic mood swing but good enough, a work place where I made my poems. Later on the horizon rose until the whole day was poisoned water and I was nothing at all just a poor little fish trapped in my own toxicity.

It was like a shade that I finally jerked from the bottom & it snapped up and it revealed something new, unchanged, but pearly.

I've been lately told that when you talk to a painter you should ask them the names of the colors of paint they use.

100

I'm telling you the name of my voice. I went to a catholic school & I hated the sound of my name. Because the form of education was, well fascistic seems too harsh militaristic too secular. I guess rote, repetitious. The nuns used flash cards. So in the middle of revery I would hear: Eileen Myles. Suddenly I was framed by the attention of the class. Half asleep drooling looking at a tree pulled back to a question of multiplication. A truth. There was the thun- derous sound of our united voices in prayer. The recitation: whither mist/fallen dew/while glow the heavens with the last steps of day. Far through thy ro- sy depths doth thou pursue thy solitary way.

Today if I sit in a circle with other humans and the leader says we'll all introduce ourselves and I say, I'm Eileen Myles I feel like my face is being split in half and I tried to keep my gaze forward, but I am compelled to turn and I look at my neighbor as if I'm asking what do you think about being, my being Eileen Myles but he is living in fear of being his own name & is begin- ning to spit it out.

When I teach I force the people to do this same embarrassment as if a community will be forged by each watching the other get vocally undressed.

Because it's the first poem, the name. All sounds are relative to my excess of eeees and the strong curling Y in my second name. Because we have names everyone has the material to begin to write a poem, a position on language, the sound of our own first, given one.

I have two ideas about poetry, received ones and I guess I have no quarrels with them. I think they've served me well. One is that there is a muse, I've got one, and she sort of sings my poems. No matter that my poems don't sound like songs or that her voice is strangely like mine. She is not me & that small gap is my freedom, that I may or may not make a poem. She feels like my Irish grandmother Nellie Reirdan, with a very soft cheek & I can't remember the sound of her voice at all. I can see the frays of her hair in the wind. She is an old strange object to me, and I am her namesake I believe. She ended her life in a mental hospital. We'd go to see her when I was five. So there's something about an old woman and a child in a sailor costume (me) and her confusing my father with her husband and me with her daughter Helen who died and this took place on the beautiful hospital grounds with loads of red & yellow tulips and later a trip to a diner for hamburgers and a dark haired waitress with bright red lips. Children had access to the small milk bottles that were intended for adults' coffee. It was charming, all of it, and then she died someplace in the nineteen fifties. I wrote a poem when I was twenty four and I couldn't believe it was me, the orderly and ironic procession of my thoughts, mundane yet passive like some kind of divine shitting.

I felt I had been seized by a form of craziness, a spell and I guess the only crazy woman I knew and I knew it was my grandmother, Nellie, she was my muse like a glass of grey wine.

We read in college about negative capability & that just makes sense to me that one would be reactive enough to talk back their whole life long. It gave me a name & now I will name everything else. It's a condition of voice, to inhabit the world. It simply occurs inside and out. The poet I know listens and speaks.

But what about things and wealth, position and jobs. What do you do?

I would like to read a poem at this point.

LOOKING OUT, A SAILOR

The clouds looked made, & perhaps
they were. An angry little shelf
for the moon to have
some influence
on. I'm dying tomorrow

my car died tonight
a glorious explosion
then clunk.

Turning pages, turning pages
coming up on midnight
when the poet died.

It was his heart
not his
head.

The girl, she was say 27
covered in tatoo
a sauce her
boyfriend
made to cover
her sins

let's say she is glad tonight
to be dead. Her name?
Lorri Jackson.

So I push on & my
dog needs

a bath — don't sell Rosie
short says the
trainer & flattered
I won't.

I remember the last
night with my
car. Came home
& called the night
watery grave. Didn't
know why. Everyone
dying around
me now. But
not yet,
not me yet.

The lights all smeared &
gooey in an incredible
downpour like Lorri's
body I could see shadows
that I think were
persons, they were
the dead &
we were
alive, yes I think
it was that
way that
last night. So lucky
I didn't hit
one.

My pooch
by my side. This
is my life
when I grow
up I thought
as a child.
In my boat with
my dog, named
what, Rosie,
she barks
driving into
the night
god, we couldn't
see a thing
but we weren't

scared. Besides
we'd had
plenty of
life.

Prayed for a
parking space.
Funny turning
in the dark
those lights
back there
are cars I think
Don't ask me
said Rosie.

But I wanted to sail
the rest of my
life. It was dumb.
I'd arrived
there was
my space.

Perfect & I pulled in
& this is the
saddest poem
I ever wrote.
What can I tell you about
sadness, the shapes
you find beneath it,
how you run from
it in your sleep,
bolting awake

early in my labors I
worked with
children, I was one
then but so
what the story goes.
Autistic kids, a
boy named
Bobby
who so loved
porcelain he leaned
his cheek on
it, a little animal
& his cool white

mama

the things I warm my
hands by are not
true, someone
who holds her
head like
that forbidding
I think
is warm

I would lay my paw
on her icy bottle,
her icy dead
cheek, her red
legs

the red light rippled
in my watery grave
if I could paint
tonight I would
be the word
that fills the silence
after modern
following something
slow, red
changing lanes
it was utterly
silent my
painting, the
dog breathing
well, relentlessly
& they had
pulled my antennae
off long ago so
deep down
there was
some music
classical,
how to say
I was having
the pivotal
moment of
my life
with a
dog, all

the silence
had led up to
here & streamers
could be
followed to
the moment
of my
death,

what kind
could I be
some kind of
poet who
followed it
along, say it's
distant &
far off, or
right next
to me
now, I
do not know
or choose
to. I saw
the world
melt all
at once

I want to
go with
everyone
waiting for
everything
to shift back
to real &
it's stranger
& stranger
now — all
of my lies don't
lie anymore.
The car dies
& I drive
on. The rain
stops. He said
I would
surely outlive
my dog &

I know
that & I
took her
home. But
everyone. No I
didn't know
that.   When
everyone
goes I
go. I'm
following
now, &
our truth
is dark

Other O Books

Return of the World, Todd Baron, $6.50

A Certain Slant of Sunlight, Ted Berrigan, $9.00

Talking in Tranquility: Interviews with Ted Berrigan, Ted Berrigan, Avenue B and O Books, $10.50

It Then, Danielle Collobert, $9.00

Candor, Alan Davies, $9.00

Turn Left in Order to Go Right, Norman Fischer, $9.00

Precisely the Point Being Made, Norman Fischer, Chax Press and O Books, $10.00

Time Rations, Benjamin Friedlander, $7.50

byt, William Fuller, $7.50

The Sugar Borders, William Fuller, $9.00

Phantom Anthems, Robert Grenier, $6.50

What I Believe   Transpiration/Transpiring   Minnesota, Robert Grenier, $24.00

The Inveterate Life, Jessica Grim, $7.50

The Quietist, Fanny Howe, $9.00

Values Chauffeur You, Andrew Levy, $9.00

Dreaming Close By, Rick London, $5.00

Abjections, Rick London, $3.50

Dissuasion Cropwds the Slow Worker, Lori Lubeski, $6.50

Catenary Odes, Ted Pearson, $5.00

(where late the sweet) BIRDS SANG, Stephen Ratcliffe, $8.00

Visible Shivers, Tom Raworth, $8.00

Kismet, Pat Reed, $8.00

Cold Heaven, Camille Roy, $9.00

O ONE/AN ANTHOLOGY, ed. Leslie Scalapino, $10.50

O TWO/AN ANTHOLOGY: What is the inside, what is outside? What is censoring? What is being censored?, ed. Leslie Scalapino, $10.50

O/3: WAR, ed. Leslie Scalapino, $4.00

Crowd and not evening or light, Leslie Scalapino, Sun & Moon and O Books, $9.00

The India Book: Essays and Translations, Andrew Schelling, $9.00

A's Dream, Aaron Shurin, $8.00

Picture of ThePicture of The Image in The Glass, Craig Watson, $8.00